THE ORIGINS OF THE QURAN

DR. MAXWELL SHIMBA

Shimba Publishing LLC

Printed in the United States of America

First Printing Edition 2024

Table of Contents

Introduction

The Quran, the holy book of Islam, is considered by Muslims to be the literal word of God (Allah) as revealed to the Prophet Muhammad over a period of approximately 23 years. This text holds a central place in the Islamic faith, providing guidance on all aspects of life, from spiritual to social matters. Understanding the origins of the Quran involves exploring its historical, theological, and literary dimensions.

The Historical Context

The Quran was revealed to Muhammad, who was born in Mecca in 570 CE. His prophetic mission began in 610 CE when he experienced his first revelation in the Cave of Hira. These revelations continued until his death in 632 CE. The period of revelation is divided into the Meccan and Medinan phases, corresponding to Muhammad's time in Mecca and after his migration (Hijra) to Medina.

The Meccan verses primarily focus on the foundations of faith, the oneness of God, the afterlife, and moral and ethical teachings. In contrast, the Medinan verses address the practical aspects of building and managing a community, including legal rulings, social justice, and conflict resolution.

The Process of Revelation

Muslims believe that the Quran was revealed in Arabic through the angel Gabriel (Jibril) to Muhammad. This process is known as Wahy (revelation). The Quran describes itself as a guidance for humanity, a clear proof of that guidance, and a criterion to distinguish right from wrong (Surah 2:185).

Muhammad's companions (Sahabah) memorized the revelations and wrote them down on various materials, including parchment, bones, and palm leaves. These fragments were later compiled into a single text during the caliphate of Abu Bakr and standardized under the third caliph, Uthman ibn Affan, to preserve the Quran's authenticity and prevent textual variations.

Compilation and Canonization

The compilation of the Quran into a single book (Mushaf) is a critical aspect of its history. After Muhammad's death, there was an urgent need to compile the Quranic text due to the deaths of several companions who had memorized it. Abu Bakr, the first caliph, initiated the collection of the Quranic text, assigning Zayd ibn Thabit, a close companion of Muhammad, to lead the task.

During Uthman's caliphate, the standardization process was completed. Multiple copies of the standardized text were produced and distributed to major Islamic centers, while other versions were ordered to be destroyed. This effort ensured the uniformity of the Quranic text, which remains unchanged to this day.

Literary and Theological Significance

The Quran is renowned for its linguistic and literary excellence. Its unique style combines prose and poetry, with rhythmic and rhyming passages that convey profound meanings and evoke deep emotional responses. The Quran's linguistic beauty is considered miraculous and inimitable (Surah 2:23).

Theologically, the Quran is the ultimate source of guidance for Muslims. It addresses various aspects of human existence, including theology, law, morality, and spirituality. It emphasizes the oneness of God (Tawhid), the importance of following God's guidance, and the accountability of individuals in the hereafter.

Interactions with Other Scriptures

The Quran acknowledges the earlier Abrahamic scriptures, including the Torah (Tawrat), the Psalms (Zabur), and the Gospel (Injil). It views itself as the final and complete revelation that confirms and supersedes previous scriptures. The Quranic narrative includes stories of previous prophets, such as Adam, Noah, Abraham, Moses, and Jesus, highlighting the continuity of divine guidance throughout human history.

Conclusion

The origins of the Quran are deeply rooted in the historical, social, and spiritual contexts of 7th-century Arabia. Its compilation and preservation reflect a meticulous process that has ensured its authenticity over centuries. The Quran's literary brilliance, coupled with its comprehensive guidance on all aspects of life, underscores its central place in the Islamic faith. Understanding the origins of the Quran provides insights into its profound impact on the lives of billions of Muslims around the world.

CHAPTER 1

An Exegesis on the Origination of the Quran

The Quran, the quintessential scripture of Islam, embodies a divine revelation bestowed upon the Prophet Muhammad over a span of approximately twenty-three years. This sacred text, revered as the verbatim word of Allah, serves as the ultimate source of guidance for Muslims worldwide. The inception and compilation of the Quran are subjects of profound theological, historical, and literary significance.

The Historical Context of Revelation

The Quranic revelations commenced in 610 CE, within the sociopolitical milieu of Mecca. Muhammad, who hailed from the respected Quraysh tribe, was forty years old when he received the initial revelation in the Cave of Hira. These revelations persisted until his demise in 632 CE, transitioning from Mecca to Medina, thereby reflecting the changing circumstances of the nascent Muslim community.

The Meccan revelations predominantly address themes of monotheism, eschatology, and ethical exhortations, aiming to fortify the nascent faith amidst a polytheistic society. Conversely, the Medinan revelations are characterized by legislative and social directives, pivotal for the establishment of an Islamic polity.

The Process of Revelation (Wahy)

The modality of the Quranic revelation, known as Wahy, signifies divine communication through the angel Gabriel (Jibril) to Muhammad. This process, as articulated in Surah 26:192-195, underscores the celestial origin of the Quran: "And indeed, the Quran is the revelation of the Lord of the worlds. The Trustworthy Spirit has brought it down upon your heart, [O Muhammad] - that you may be of the warners - in a clear Arabic language." The Quranic text itself is seen as both a guidance (Huda) and a criterion (Furqan), delineating the path of righteousness and distinguishing truth from falsehood (Surah 2:185).

Muhammad's companions (Sahabah) played a crucial role in preserving these revelations. They meticulously memorized and documented the Quranic verses on various materials, ensuring their transmission to future generations. This practice is corroborated by the Hadith, wherein Muhammad emphasized the importance of accurate preservation: "Do not write down anything from me except the Quran. Whoever writes anything other than the Quran, let him erase it" (Sahih Muslim).

Compilation and Canonization of the Quran

The compilation of the Quran into a single codex (Mushaf) is a seminal event in Islamic history. Following Muhammad's death, the need to consolidate the Quranic text became paramount, particularly due to the martyrdom of many Quranic memorizers (Hafiz) in the Battle of Yamama. The first caliph, Abu Bakr, commissioned Zayd ibn Thabit, a prominent scribe, to collect the Quranic verses. This effort was aimed at preserving the Quranic integrity and ensuring its transmission.

The standardization of the Quranic text was later completed during the caliphate of Uthman ibn Affan. To prevent divergent recitations, Uthman ordered the production of standardized copies and distributed them to various Islamic territories, while other versions were systematically destroyed. This process is documented in Sahih Bukhari: "Uthman sent to every Muslim province one copy of what they had copied, and ordered that all the other Quranic materials, whether written in fragmentary manuscripts or whole copies, be burnt" (Sahih Bukhari).

The Literary and Theological Significance

The Quran is celebrated for its unparalleled literary excellence, characterized by its unique style that amalgamates prose and poetry. The rhythmic and phonetic qualities of the Quran, coupled with its profound thematic content, render it inimitable. Surah 2:23 presents a challenge to skeptics: "And if you are in doubt about what We have sent down upon Our Servant [Muhammad], then produce a surah the like thereof and call upon your witnesses other than Allah, if you should be truthful."

Theologically, the Quran is the epitome of divine guidance. It elucidates the principles of Tawhid (the oneness of Allah), delineates the moral and ethical framework for human conduct, and provides comprehensive legislation on social, economic, and political matters. The Quran's holistic guidance is aimed at fostering a just and equitable society, rooted in divine wisdom.

Conclusion

The origination and preservation of the Quran are pivotal to understanding its profound impact on Islamic civilization. The meticulous compilation and standardization efforts reflect the unwavering commitment of the early Muslim community to safeguard the divine message. The Quran's theological profundity and literary brilliance continue to inspire and guide billions of Muslims, underscoring its timeless relevance and sanctity.

References:

1. Surah 26:192-195 - The celestial origin of the Quran.
2. Surah 2:185 - The Quran as guidance and a criterion.
3. Sahih Muslim - Preservation of the Quranic text.
4. Sahih Bukhari - Compilation and standardization of the Quran.
5. Surah 2:23 - The inimitable literary excellence of the Quran.

In Islamic orthodoxy, questioning the divine authorship of the Quran is tantamount to blasphemy, punishable by death in some interpretations. The Quran is revered as the ultimate divine revelation, superseding all other religious texts. However, the human spirit, ever inquisitive, naturally inclines toward skepticism and inquiry. My own journey of doubt began in childhood, during rote memorization of Quranic verses under the strict tutelage of a local Hujur (religious teacher). The experience, marred by corporal punishment, fostered a deep aversion to the Quranic recitation and an inherent mistrust of religious authorities.

My investigations led me to uncover substantial evidence within the Quran, Hadith, and Sirah (biographical accounts of Muhammad) that point to a multifaceted authorship. The claim that the Quran is the verbatim word of Allah appears increasingly untenable when examined in light of historical and literary analyses. Instead, it becomes evident that numerous individuals contributed to its creation.

The Pagan Origins of Muhammad

Muhammad's early life was steeped in paganism, a fact often overlooked or downplayed by traditional Islamic narratives. His parents, Abdullah and Amina, were idolaters, worshipping numerous deities. This is substantiated by Hisham ibn al-Kalbi's work, "Kitab al-Asnam" (The Book of Idols), where he recounts Muhammad's admission of past pagan practices: "We have been told that the Apostle of God once mentioned al-Uzza, saying, 'I have offered a white sheep to al-Uzza while I was a follower of the religion of my people.'"

Initially, Muhammad even acknowledged the deities of the Quraysh, recognizing them as intermediaries to Allah. Hisham ibn al-Kalbi further narrates the Quraysh's invocation to their deities, including al-Lat, al-Uzza, and Manat, which were considered daughters of Allah (Quran 53:19-23). These deities were integral to the religious practices of the Quraysh, reflecting the polytheistic environment in which Muhammad was raised.

As Muhammad matured and engaged with the intellectual milieu of his time, particularly the annual assembly of poets at Ukaz, he began to reject idol worship. Influenced by the monotheistic teachings of Jews and Christians, he initially adopted "Ar-Rahman" (the Merciful) as the name for God, reflecting a term used by Jews in Talmudic texts. This caused confusion among the Meccans, who were unfamiliar with this appellation outside the context of a deity worshipped in Yemen (Ibn Sa'd, "Kitab al-Tabaqat al-Kabir").

Literary Influences and Contributions

The literary landscape of pre-Islamic Arabia was dominated by poets whose works were revered and memorized. Among these poets, Imrul Qays stands out as a seminal figure whose verses profoundly influenced the early Quranic text. His poetry, known for its eloquence and emotive power, resonated deeply with the Arab psyche. Muhammad, well-versed in these poetic traditions, drew inspiration from Imrul Qays and other poets, incorporating their stylistic elements into the Quran.

W. St. Clair-Tisdall, in his analysis of the origins of the Quran, notes the striking similarities between the Quranic verses and the poetry of Imrul Qays. For instance, the opening verses of Surah 54 (Al-Qamar) bear resemblance to Imrul Qays's poems, suggesting a direct literary influence. This challenges the claim of divine origin, proposing instead a human literary tradition as the source.

The Role of Hanifism and Other Religious Traditions

Hanifism, a monotheistic movement predating Islam, played a crucial role in shaping Muhammad's theological outlook. Zayd b. Amr, a prominent Hanifite, rejected idolatry and preached the worship of a single God. His teachings significantly influenced Muhammad, who later adapted these ideas into the framework of Islam. The Quran reflects this influence, with numerous verses echoing Hanifite monotheism (Quran 3:67).

Moreover, the Sabean practices of ritual prayer and fasting were integrated into Islamic rituals, demonstrating the Quran's syncretic nature. The adoption of these pre-Islamic religious practices further undermines the notion of the Quran as a purely divine revelation, highlighting its composite and evolutionary character.

Conclusion

In conclusion, the Quran emerges not as a singular divine dictation but as a tapestry woven from diverse human contributions and pre-existing religious traditions. Muhammad, far from being a passive recipient of divine messages, played an active role in shaping and editing the text. This reevaluation invites a more nuanced understanding of the Quran, recognizing it as a product of historical, cultural, and literary contexts. This perspective not only challenges traditional Islamic doctrine but also enriches our appreciation of the Quran as a complex and multifaceted text.

References:

1. Quran 53:19-23 - Discussing the daughters of Allah.

2. Quran 93:7 - "And He found you lost and guided [you]."

3. Quran 12:3 - "Indeed, We relate to you, [O Muhammad], the best of stories in what We have revealed to you of this Quran although you were, before it, among the unaware."

4. Ibn Sa'd, "Kitab al-Tabaqat al-Kabir" - Historical accounts of Muhammad's life.

5. Hisham ibn al-Kalbi, "Kitab al-Asnam" - Details on pre-Islamic Arabian deities.

6. W. St. Clair-Tisdall, "The Origins of the Koran" - Comparative analysis of Quranic verses and pre-Islamic poetry.

CHAPTER 2

The Contributions of Key Figures in the Quran's Composition

The Role of Imrul Qays

Imrul Qays, an illustrious poet of pre-Islamic Arabia, stands as a paramount figure whose influence permeated the early Quranic text. His poetry, celebrated for its profound emotional depth and linguistic elegance, left an indelible mark on the literary traditions of the region. It is within this cultural milieu that Muhammad, familiar with Imrul Qays's works, found inspiration.

The resemblance between certain Quranic verses and the poetry of Imrul Qays is striking. For example, the verses of Surah 54 (Al-Qamar) bear a remarkable similarity to the poetic style of Imrul Qays, suggesting a direct literary influence. W. St. Clair-Tisdall, in his comparative analysis, underscores this connection, arguing that the rhythmic and thematic elements in these verses are reflective of Imrul Qays's poetic legacy. Such parallels challenge the notion of the Quran's divine origin, pointing instead to a human literary tradition that predates Islam.

Zayd b. Amr: The Hanifite Influence

Zayd b. Amr b. Naufal, an ardent preacher of Hanifism, played a crucial role in shaping Muhammad's theological framework. Hanifism, a monotheistic movement that rejected idolatry and emphasized the worship of one God, significantly influenced Muhammad's early religious outlook. Zayd's teachings, which promoted a pure form of monotheism devoid of pagan practices, resonated deeply with Muhammad, who later incorporated these principles into the nascent Islamic faith.

The Quran itself acknowledges the Hanifite influence, as seen in verses that underscore the monotheistic message preached by Zayd. For instance, Quran 3:67 states, "Ibrahim was neither a Jew nor a Christian, but he was one inclining toward truth, a Muslim [submitting to Allah]. And he was not of the polytheists." This verse reflects the Hanifite emphasis on pure monotheism and positions Ibrahim as a precursor to Muhammad's message.

Salman the Persian: The Cross-Cultural Catalyst

Salman the Persian, a companion of Muhammad and a pivotal figure in early Islamic history, brought a wealth of cross-cultural knowledge to the formation of the Quran. His background as a Zoroastrian, followed by his conversion to Christianity and eventually Islam, provided a unique confluence of religious traditions that enriched the Quranic text. Salman's familiarity with Persian, Christian, and Zoroastrian teachings allowed for a broader incorporation of religious concepts into the Quran.

Hadith literature acknowledges Salman's significant contributions. In Sahih Bukhari (Book 58, Hadith 160), it is recorded that Muhammad said, "Salman is one of us, the people of the (Prophet's) Household." This recognition highlights Salman's integral role within the early Muslim community and his influence on the development of Islamic doctrine.

The Christian Monk Bahira

Bahira, a Nestorian Christian monk, is another figure whose interactions with Muhammad are believed to have influenced the Quran. According to Islamic tradition, Bahira recognized signs of prophethood in the young Muhammad during a caravan journey to Syria. This encounter, detailed in early biographical accounts, is thought to have left a lasting impression on Muhammad, introducing him to Christian theological concepts.

The Quranic narrative bears traces of Christian influence, particularly in its depiction of Jesus (Isa) and the Virgin Mary (Maryam). Verses such as Quran 3:45-47, which recount the annunciation to Mary, mirror the accounts found in the Christian Gospels. This intertextuality suggests that Muhammad's exposure to

Christian teachings, possibly through figures like Bahira, informed his portrayal of biblical characters and events.

Waraqa bin Nawfal: The Familial Mentor

Waraqa bin Nawfal, a cousin of Muhammad's first wife Khadijah, was a learned Christian who played a mentoring role in Muhammad's early prophetic career. Waraqa's extensive knowledge of the Christian scriptures and his supportive stance towards Muhammad's mission provided a vital source of encouragement and guidance.

In Sahih Bukhari (Book 1, Hadith 3), it is narrated that Khadijah took Muhammad to Waraqa after the first revelation. Waraqa, upon hearing the account, affirmed Muhammad's prophetic experience, stating, "This is the same one who keeps the secrets (angel Gabriel) whom Allah had sent to Moses." This validation from Waraqa, rooted in his Christian understanding, underscores the interconnectedness of the Quranic revelation with pre-existing religious traditions.

Ubayy b. Ka'b: The Scribe

Ubayy b. Ka'b, one of Muhammad's prominent scribes, was instrumental in the compilation and preservation of the Quranic text. His role as a scribe placed him at the forefront of recording the revelations, ensuring their accuracy and consistency. Ubayy's meticulous work is recognized in various hadiths, including those found in Sahih Muslim (Book 31, Hadith 6047), where Muhammad is reported to have said, "The most proficient person in the recitation of the Book of Allah is Ubayy b. Ka'b."

The precision and care with which Ubayy transcribed the revelations were crucial in establishing the textual integrity of the Quran. His contributions highlight the collaborative nature of the Quran's compilation, involving multiple individuals dedicated to preserving the divine message.

Conclusion

The Quran, far from being a monolithic divine dictation, emerges as a complex text shaped by the contributions of various individuals and cultural influences. Figures such as Imrul Qays, Zayd b. Amr, Salman the Persian, Bahira, Waraqa bin Nawfal, and Ubayy b. Ka'b played pivotal roles in its composition and transmission. Their diverse backgrounds and religious experiences enriched the Quranic narrative, embedding within it a tapestry of interwoven traditions and teachings.

This reexamination of the Quran's authorship invites a more nuanced understanding of its origins, acknowledging the human elements that contributed to its formation. It challenges traditional notions of divine exclusivity, proposing instead a collaborative process that reflects the dynamic interplay of historical, cultural, and theological factors.

References:

1. Quran 3:67 - Discussing the monotheism of Ibrahim.
2. Sahih Bukhari, Book 58, Hadith 160 - Acknowledgment of Salman the Persian.

3. Quran 3:45-47 - Annunciation to Mary.

4. Sahih Bukhari, Book 1, Hadith 3 - Waraqa bin Nawfal's affirmation of Muhammad's prophethood.

5. Sahih Muslim, Book 31, Hadith 6047 - Ubayy b. Ka'b's proficiency in Quranic recitation.

CHAPTER 3
The Influence of Pagan and Other Religious Practices on the Quran

The Pagan Heritage of the Quran

Muhammad's upbringing in a pagan society profoundly influenced the early development of his religious thought. Born into the Quraysh tribe, which venerated a pantheon of deities, Muhammad's early exposure to polytheism played a pivotal role in shaping his initial theological framework. The Quran itself contains several references to pre-Islamic practices and deities, indicating a complex process of religious transformation and assimilation.

Hisham ibn al-Kalbi's "Kitab al-Asnam" provides a crucial insight into Muhammad's pagan origins. The text recounts Muhammad's acknowledgment of having offered sacrifices to the deity al-Uzza during his youth: "I have offered a white sheep to al-Uzza while I was a follower of the religion of my people" (Hisham ibn al-Kalbi, "Kitab al-Asnam," p.17). This admission underscores the deep-rooted influence of pagan rituals on Muhammad's early life and highlights the significant transition from polytheism to monotheism that he later championed.

Adaptation of Pagan Rituals

The incorporation of certain pagan rituals into Islamic practice is a testament to the syncretic nature of early Islam. One of the most striking examples is the ritual of the Hajj, which retains several elements of pre-Islamic pilgrimage traditions. The circumambulation of the Kaaba (Tawaf), the kissing of the Black Stone (Hajr al-Aswad), and the running between the hills of Safa and Marwah (Sa'i) are all practices that predate Islam and were integral to the pagan rites of the Quraysh.

The Quran acknowledges these rituals, recontextualizing them within an Islamic framework. For instance, Quran 2:158 states, "Indeed, Safa and Marwah are among the symbols of Allah. So whoever makes Hajj to the House or performs Umrah - there is no blame upon him for walking between them. And whoever volunteers good - indeed, Allah is appreciative and Knowing." This verse effectively sanctifies the pre-Islamic practice of Sa'i, incorporating it into the new monotheistic religion.

The Sabean Influence

The Sabeans, an ancient religious community mentioned in the Quran, also contributed significantly to the formation of Islamic rituals. The practices of the Sabeans, particularly their devotion to regular prayer and fasting, were adapted and integrated into Islamic worship. The Quranic reference to the Sabeans in Surah 2:62 highlights their recognized status among the "People of the Book": "Indeed, those who believed and those who were Jews or Christians or Sabeans - those [among them] who believed in Allah and the Last Day and did righteousness - will have their reward with their Lord, and no fear will there be concerning them, nor will they grieve."

The five daily prayers (Salat) and the fasting during the month of Ramadan bear similarities to Sabean practices. Historical accounts suggest that the Sabeans engaged in regular, structured prayer and observed periods of fasting, rituals that were subsequently incorporated into Islamic worship with specific modifications and contextual adaptations.

Jewish and Christian Elements

Islamic tradition acknowledges the significant influence of Jewish and Christian teachings on the Quran. Muhammad's interactions with Jewish and Christian communities, as well as his exposure to their scriptures and religious practices, are well documented in Islamic sources. The Quran itself references numerous biblical narratives and characters, reinterpreting them within an Islamic context.

For example, the Quranic account of the creation and the story of Adam and Eve closely parallel the biblical narrative found in Genesis. Surah 2:30-34 details the creation of Adam, the command to the angels to prostrate before him, and the subsequent disobedience of Iblis (Satan), mirroring the themes present in the Book of Genesis. Additionally, the Quranic depiction of Jesus (Isa) and his mother Mary (Maryam) draws heavily on Christian sources, with Surah 19 (Maryam) providing a detailed account of the annunciation and birth of Jesus, akin to the Gospel accounts.

The Role of Hadith in Shaping Islamic Practices

The Hadith literature, comprising the sayings and actions of Muhammad, plays a crucial role in shaping Islamic law and practice. These traditions offer insights into the Prophet's interpretations and applications of Quranic teachings, further elucidating the religious and cultural milieu in which Islam developed.

One significant example is the Hadith's role in formalizing the five daily prayers. While the Quran mentions the importance of regular prayer, it is through the Hadith that the specific times and procedures for Salat are detailed. In Sahih Bukhari (Book 10, Hadith 506), it is narrated that Muhammad said, "Pray as you have seen me praying." This directive, preserved through Hadith, underscores the centrality of the Prophet's example in defining Islamic worship practices.

Conclusion

The Quran, while regarded as the ultimate divine revelation by Muslims, is deeply rooted in the cultural, religious, and historical context of its time. The incorporation of pagan rituals, the influence of Sabean practices, and the adaptation of Jewish and Christian teachings all point to a syncretic process that shaped the early development of Islam. By examining these influences, one gains a more nuanced understanding of the Quran's composition and the complex interplay of factors that contributed to its formation.

This reexamination challenges the traditional view of the Quran as a purely divine text, proposing instead a multifaceted origin that reflects the rich tapestry of human religious experience. It invites scholars and believers alike to explore the profound connections between Islam and the broader religious traditions that preceded it.

References:

1. Hisham ibn al-Kalbi, "Kitab al-Asnam," p.17.
2. Quran 2:158 - Rituals of Hajj.
3. Quran 2:62 - Reference to the Sabeans.
4. Sahih Bukhari, Book 10, Hadith 506 - Formalization of the five daily prayers.
5. Quran 2:30-34 - Creation of Adam narrative.
6. Quran 19 - Account of Jesus and Mary.

CHAPTER 4

The Evolution of Muhammad's Theological Thought

The Transition from Paganism to Monotheism

Muhammad's journey from paganism to monotheism reflects a complex evolution of theological thought, influenced by his exposure to various religious traditions and intellectual milieus. Born into a pagan society, Muhammad's early life was characterized by the worship of multiple deities, a practice deeply ingrained in the Quraysh tribe. This initial phase is crucial for understanding the transformative process that led Muhammad to advocate for the worship of a singular, omnipotent deity.

The Quran itself acknowledges this period of transition. In Surah 93:6-7, it is stated, "Did He not find you an orphan and give [you] refuge? And He found you lost and guided [you]." These verses highlight Muhammad's state of spiritual disorientation before receiving divine guidance, reflecting his gradual shift from polytheism to monotheism.

The Intellectual Influence of Hanifism

Hanifism, a pre-Islamic monotheistic movement, played a pivotal role in shaping Muhammad's emerging religious consciousness. The Hanifs, who rejected idolatry and espoused the worship of a singular God, provided an ideological framework that resonated with Muhammad. Among the notable Hanifs was Zayd b. Amr b. Naufal, whose teachings left a lasting impression on Muhammad.

The Quranic verses often reflect Hanifite principles. For example, Quran 6:79 states, "Indeed, I have turned my face toward He who created the heavens and the earth, inclining toward truth, and I am not of those who associate others with Allah." This declaration of monotheistic faith is indicative of the Hanifite influence on Muhammad's theology, emphasizing a pure and uncompromising monotheism.

The Role of Revelation and Prophetic Experience

Muhammad's prophetic experience, marked by the reception of revelations, further solidified his transition from paganism to monotheism. The first revelation, traditionally believed to be the opening verses of Surah 96 (Al-Alaq), initiated a profound transformation in Muhammad's spiritual and intellectual outlook. The

Quran describes this pivotal moment in Surah 96:1-5, "Recite in the name of your Lord who created – Created man from a clinging substance. Recite, and your Lord is the most Generous – Who taught by the pen – Taught man that which he knew not."

This experience of divine communication reinforced Muhammad's conviction in a singular, all-encompassing deity, steering him away from the polytheistic practices of his youth. It also marked the beginning of his mission to propagate this monotheistic message, a task that was met with both acceptance and resistance within his community.

Integration of Jewish and Christian Narratives

Muhammad's interactions with Jewish and Christian communities further enriched his theological perspective. These encounters introduced him to biblical narratives and theological concepts, which he subsequently integrated into the Quranic text. The Quranic portrayal of prophets such as Moses (Musa) and Jesus (Isa) reflects a deep engagement with Judeo-Christian traditions.

For instance, the Quranic account of Moses' encounter with Pharaoh parallels the biblical narrative found in the Book of Exodus. In Surah 7:103-137, the story is retold with a focus on Moses' role as a divinely appointed leader who challenges the tyranny of Pharaoh, emphasizing themes of liberation and divine justice. Similarly, the depiction of Jesus in Surah 19:16-34 aligns with the Gospel accounts, highlighting his miraculous birth and prophetic mission.

The Hadith as a Source of Theological Elaboration

The Hadith literature, comprising the sayings and actions of Muhammad, serves as a crucial source for understanding the evolution of his theological thought. These traditions provide insights into how Muhammad interpreted and applied Quranic teachings, offering a more nuanced view of his religious and ethical principles.

One notable example is the Hadith's elaboration on the concept of Tawhid (the oneness of God). In Sahih Muslim (Book 1, Hadith 1), it is narrated that Muhammad said, "The best supplication is the supplication on the Day of Arafah, and the best of what I and the prophets before me have said is: There is no god but Allah, alone, without partner." This Hadith underscores the centrality of monotheism in Muhammad's message, reflecting his unwavering commitment to the principle of divine unity.

Conclusion

Muhammad's theological journey from paganism to monotheism represents a dynamic and multifaceted process, influenced by various religious traditions and intellectual currents. The integration of Hanifite monotheism, Jewish and Christian narratives, and the profound impact of divine revelation collectively shaped his religious outlook. The Hadith literature further elucidates his theological principles, offering a comprehensive understanding of his mission to establish a monotheistic faith.

This exploration of Muhammad's evolving theological thought invites a deeper appreciation of the complex interplay between religious traditions and the development of Islamic doctrine. It challenges simplistic narratives and highlights the rich tapestry of influences that contributed to the formation of early Islam.

References:

1. Quran 93:6-7 - Muhammad's spiritual transition.
2. Quran 6:79 - Declaration of monotheistic faith.
3. Quran 96:1-5 - The first revelation.
4. Quran 7:103-137 - The story of Moses and Pharaoh.
5. Quran 19:16-34 - The depiction of Jesus.
6. Sahih Muslim, Book 1, Hadith 1 - Elaboration on Tawhid.

Theological Foundations of the Quran

The theological underpinnings of the Quran are rooted in the principle of Tawhid, the oneness and absolute unity of Allah. This fundamental concept is reiterated throughout the Quran, serving as the cornerstone of Islamic faith. Surah 112:1-4 succinctly encapsulates this doctrine: "Say, 'He is Allah, [Who is] One, Allah, the Eternal Refuge. He neither begets nor is born, nor is there to Him any equivalent.'" This declaration affirms the uniqueness and indivisibility of Allah, distinguishing Islamic monotheism from other religious traditions.

The Quran also delineates the concept of Risalah (prophethood), emphasizing the role of prophets as intermediaries who convey divine guidance to humanity. The Quran recognizes a succession of prophets, including Adam, Noah, Abraham, Moses, and Jesus, culminating in Muhammad, the final prophet. Surah 33:40 states, "Muhammad is not the father of [any] one of your men, but [he is] the Messenger of Allah and seal of the prophets. And ever is Allah, of all things, Knowing." This verse underscores Muhammad's unique position as the last prophet, entrusted with delivering the final and complete revelation.

Literary Excellence and Inimitability

The Quran is renowned for its unparalleled literary quality, characterized by its unique linguistic style that blends prose and poetry. This distinctive style, known as Saj', is marked by rhythmic and phonetic harmony, which enhances the recitability and memorability of the text. The Quran's linguistic beauty is considered a miraculous attribute, reinforcing its divine origin. Surah 17:88 poses a challenge to skeptics: "Say, 'If mankind and the jinn gathered in order to produce the like of this Quran, they could not produce the like of it, even if they were to each other assistants.'"

The inimitability (I'jaz) of the Quran is a central tenet in Islamic theology, asserting that the Quran's literary and rhetorical features are beyond human capability to replicate. This belief is supported by numerous verses that invite humanity to produce a single chapter comparable to the Quran. Surah 2:23-24 challenges: "And if you are in doubt about what We have sent down upon Our Servant [Muhammad], then produce a surah the like thereof and call upon your witnesses other than Allah, if you should be truthful. But if you do not - and you will never be able to - then fear the Fire, whose fuel is men and stones, prepared for the disbelievers."

Thematic Unity and Structure

The Quran exhibits a thematic unity, despite being revealed over two decades. Its chapters (Surahs) and verses (Ayahs) address various aspects of life, including theology, law, morality, and guidance for personal and communal conduct. The Quran's structure, while non-linear, is meticulously organized to reflect its comprehensive and multifaceted message.

One of the predominant themes is the call to faith and righteousness. The Quran repeatedly urges believers to uphold justice, compassion, and ethical conduct. Surah 16:90 exemplifies this exhortation: "Indeed, Allah orders justice and good conduct and giving to relatives and forbids immorality and bad conduct and oppression. He admonishes you that perhaps you will be reminded." This verse encapsulates the Quranic vision of a just and moral society, grounded in divine guidance.

Intertextuality and Historical Narratives

The Quran engages in a rich intertextual dialogue with earlier scriptures, particularly the Torah and the Gospel. It acknowledges the revelations given to previous prophets and positions itself as a continuation and culmination of these divine messages. Surah 5:48 states, "And We have revealed to you, [O Muhammad], the Book in truth, confirming that which preceded it of the Scripture and as a criterion over it. So judge between them by what Allah has revealed and do not follow their inclinations away from what has come to you of the truth."

Historical narratives play a significant role in the Quran, serving both didactic and theological purposes. Stories of past prophets and communities are recounted to illustrate moral lessons and divine justice. For instance, the story of Joseph (Yusuf) in Surah 12 provides profound insights into patience, forgiveness, and divine providence: "And they sold him for a reduced price - a few dirhams - and they were, concerning him, of those content with little. And he said, 'Indeed, I am Joseph, and this is my brother. Allah has certainly favored us. Indeed, he who fears Allah and is patient, then indeed, Allah does not allow to be lost the reward of those who do good.'"

Legal and Ethical Guidance

The Quran serves as a comprehensive legal and ethical guide, outlining principles and regulations that govern various aspects of personal and communal life. Its legal injunctions cover areas such as worship, family law, criminal justice, and economic transactions. The ethical teachings of the Quran emphasize virtues such as honesty, humility, patience, and generosity.

The Hadith literature complements the Quran by providing detailed explanations and applications of its legal and ethical directives. For instance, the Hadith recorded in Sahih Muslim (Book 32, Hadith 6251) emphasizes the importance of compassion: "He who does not show mercy to others will not be shown mercy." This Hadith underscores the Quranic principle of mercy and kindness, which is fundamental to Islamic ethics.

Conclusion

The theological and literary dimensions of the Quran underscore its profound impact on Islamic thought and civilization. Its articulation of monotheism, prophethood, and divine guidance forms the bedrock of Islamic theology, while its literary excellence and thematic unity highlight its miraculous nature. The Quran's engagement with historical narratives and intertextual references enriches its message, providing timeless lessons for humanity. Through its comprehensive legal and ethical framework, the Quran continues to guide and inspire Muslims around the world.

References:

1. Surah 112:1-4 - Declaration of divine unity.
2. Surah 33:40 - Muhammad as the final prophet.
3. Surah 17:88 - Inimitability of the Quran.
4. Surah 2:23-24 - Challenge to produce a surah like the Quran.

5. Surah 16:90 - Exhortation to justice and good conduct.

6. Surah 5:48 - Quran as a confirmation of earlier scriptures.

7. Surah 12 - Story of Joseph.

8. Sahih Muslim, Book 32, Hadith 6251 - Importance of compassion.

CHAPTER 5

The Literary Craftsmanship of the Quran

The Interplay of the Quran with Pre-Islamic and Abrahamic Traditions

The Syncretic Context of Pre-Islamic Arabia

The Quran emerged within the intricate religious and cultural milieu of pre-Islamic Arabia, a region characterized by a rich tapestry of polytheistic practices, monotheistic influences, and diverse tribal traditions. Understanding this syncretic context is crucial to appreciating the Quran's unique theological and literary dimensions.

Pre-Islamic Arabia was dominated by the worship of numerous deities, with the Kaaba in Mecca serving as a central sanctuary housing various idols. The Quran acknowledges this polytheistic backdrop and vehemently opposes it, advocating for the worship of the singular, omnipotent Allah. Surah 6:19 asserts, "Say, 'What thing is greatest in testimony?' Say, 'Allah is witness between me and you. And this Quran was revealed to me that I may warn you thereby and whomever it reaches. Do you truly testify that with Allah there are other deities?' Say, 'I will not testify [with you].' Say, 'Indeed, He is but one God, and indeed, I am free of what you associate [with Him].'"

The Influence of Abrahamic Traditions

The Quran positions itself as a continuation and culmination of the Abrahamic traditions, recognizing and affirming the scriptures revealed to previous prophets, including the Torah (Tawrat) and the Gospel (Injil). This intertextual relationship underscores the Quran's role in reaffirming the core tenets of monotheism, prophethood, and divine guidance.

Surah 3:3-4 elucidates this connection: "He has sent down upon you, [O Muhammad], the Book in truth, confirming what was before it. And He revealed the Torah and the Gospel. Before as guidance for the people. And He revealed the Criterion [i.e., the Quran]." This passage highlights the Quran's function as both a validator and a final arbiter of previous revelations, positioning it within the broader continuum of divine communication.

The Hadith literature reinforces this integrative approach. In Sahih Bukhari (Book 55, Hadith 649), the Prophet Muhammad is reported to have said, "Both in this world and the Hereafter, I am the nearest of all the people to Jesus, the son of Mary. The prophets are paternal brothers; their mothers are different, but their religion is one."

This Hadith underscores the shared spiritual lineage of the Abrahamic prophets, emphasizing the Quran's role in perpetuating this legacy.

Reinterpretation and Recontextualization of Biblical Narratives

The Quran engages in a dynamic reinterpretation and recontextualization of Biblical narratives, embedding them within its own theological framework. This approach serves to reinforce the Quran's central messages while distinguishing its unique perspective on these ancient stories.

One prominent example is the Quranic account of Moses (Musa) and Pharaoh, which mirrors yet diverges from the Biblical Exodus narrative. In Surah 28:3-4, the Quran states, "We recite to you from the news of Moses and Pharaoh in truth for a people who believe. Indeed, Pharaoh exalted himself in the land and made its people into factions, oppressing a sector among them, slaughtering their [newborn] sons and keeping their females alive. Indeed, he was of the corrupters." This rendition not only reiterates the themes of divine justice and deliverance but also serves to highlight the moral and spiritual lessons pertinent to the Quran's audience.

Integration of Pre-Islamic Poetry and Rhetoric

The Quran's linguistic and rhetorical mastery is partly attributable to its integration of pre-Islamic poetic forms and conventions. The eloquence and stylistic sophistication of the Quran resonate deeply with the established literary traditions of pre-Islamic Arabia, enhancing its impact and memorability.

Pre-Islamic poetry, known for its elaborate metaphors, vivid imagery, and rhythmic cadence, profoundly influenced the Quran's linguistic style. The Quran's use of Saj' (rhymed prose) and its employment of metaphors and allegories reflect this literary heritage. For instance, Surah 91:1-10 exemplifies the Quran's poetic elegance: "By the sun and its brightness. And [by] the moon when it follows it. And [by] the day when it displays it. And [by] the night when it covers it. And [by] the sky and He who constructed it. And [by] the earth and He who spread it. And [by] the soul and He who proportioned it. And inspired it [with discernment of] its wickedness and its righteousness. He has succeeded who purifies it, and he has failed who instills it [with corruption]."

The Ethical and Legal Continuities

The Quran's ethical and legal precepts often reflect a continuation and refinement of pre-existing norms and practices. By endorsing and modifying certain aspects of pre-Islamic Arabian customs, the Quran establishes a coherent and pragmatic legal framework that addresses the needs and realities of its audience.

For instance, the Quran's regulations on marriage, commerce, and social justice build upon existing Arabian traditions while infusing them with ethical rigor and divine sanction. Surah 4:3 addresses the practice of polygamy, setting conditions to ensure justice and equity: "And if you fear that you will not deal justly with the orphan girls, then marry those that please you of [other] women, two or three or four. But if you fear that you will not be just, then [marry only] one or those your right hand possesses. That is more suitable that you may not incline [to injustice]."

The Hadith literature further explicates these ethical continuities. In Sahih Muslim (Book 16, Hadith 4127), the Prophet Muhammad states, "Whoever cheats us is not one of us." This Hadith reinforces the Quranic injunctions against deceit and fraud, emphasizing the moral integrity that Islam seeks to cultivate in all spheres of life.

Conclusion

The interplay between the Quran and pre-Islamic as well as Abrahamic traditions underscores the Quran's role as a transformative yet integrative text. By reinterpreting and recontextualizing earlier narratives, integrating pre-Islamic literary forms, and refining existing ethical and legal norms, the Quran presents a coherent and compelling vision of divine guidance. This intricate synthesis not only affirms the Quran's theological profundity and literary brilliance but also highlights its enduring relevance and applicability.

References:

1. Surah 6:19 - The opposition to polytheism and affirmation of monotheism.
2. Surah 3:3-4 - The Quran as a continuation and culmination of previous scriptures.
3. Sahih Bukhari, Book 55, Hadith 649 - The shared spiritual lineage of the Abrahamic prophets.
4. Surah 28:3-4 - The Quranic account of Moses and Pharaoh.
5. Surah 91:1-10 - The Quran's poetic elegance.

6. Surah 4:3 - Regulations on marriage to ensure justice and equity.

7. Sahih Muslim, Book 16, Hadith 4127 - The ethical injunctions against deceit and fraud.

The Poetic and Prosaic Elements

The Quran's literary composition is a masterful blend of poetic and prosaic elements, reflecting the rich oral tradition of pre-Islamic Arabia. Its rhythmic cadence, intricate rhyme schemes, and eloquent expressions demonstrate a high level of linguistic artistry. This sophisticated use of language not only facilitated the memorization and recitation of the Quran but also enhanced its emotional and spiritual impact on its audience.

The Quran itself acknowledges its inimitable literary quality, challenging skeptics to produce a text of comparable eloquence. In Surah 2:23, it is stated, "And if you are in doubt about what We have sent down upon Our Servant [Muhammad], then produce a surah the like thereof and call upon your witnesses other than Allah, if you should be truthful." This verse underscores the Quran's claim to unmatched linguistic excellence, positioning it as a divine miracle.

The Integration of Pre-Islamic Poetic Traditions

The Quran's literary style is deeply rooted in the pre-Islamic poetic tradition, which was characterized by a profound appreciation for eloquence and verbal artistry. Poets such as Imrul Qays and Labid set the standard for linguistic excellence, and their influence is evident in the Quran's use of metaphors, similes, and vivid imagery.

For instance, the depiction of the Day of Judgment in Surah 99:1-8 (Al-Zalzalah) employs a dramatic and evocative language reminiscent of pre-Islamic poetry: "When the earth is shaken with its [final] earthquake and the earth discharges its burdens, and man says,

'What is [wrong] with it?' That Day, it will report its news because your Lord has commanded it." This passage illustrates the Quran's ability to convey profound theological concepts through powerful and poetic imagery.

The Role of Divine Inspiration and Human Agency

While the Quran is regarded by Muslims as the verbatim word of Allah, transmitted to Muhammad through the angel Gabriel (Jibril), the role of human agency in its compilation and preservation cannot be overlooked. The Quranic revelation was received over a period of 23 years, during which Muhammad's companions (Sahabah) played a crucial role in recording and preserving the text.

The Hadith literature provides numerous accounts of this process. In Sahih Bukhari (Book 61, Hadith 509), it is narrated that Muhammad instructed his scribes, including Zayd ibn Thabit, to write down the revelations. This collaborative effort ensured the accurate transmission of the Quranic text, highlighting the interplay between divine inspiration and human agency.

The Compilation and Canonization of the Quran

The process of compiling and canonizing the Quran involved significant scholarly effort and meticulous attention to detail. After Muhammad's death, the need to compile the Quran into a single, coherent text became evident, particularly in light of the deaths of many of the Prophet's companions who had memorized large portions of the Quran.

The Caliph Abu Bakr initiated the first compilation, entrusting Zayd ibn Thabit with the task. This effort was later consolidated during the caliphate of Uthman ibn Affan, who commissioned the production of a standardized text to prevent divergent recitations. The Hadith in Sahih Bukhari (Book 61, Hadith 510) records Uthman's directive to Zayd ibn Thabit and other scribes to compile the Quran: "Uthman sent to every Muslim province one copy of what they had copied, and ordered that all the other Quranic materials, whether written in fragmentary manuscripts or whole copies, be burnt."

The Intertextuality of the Quran

The Quran's intertextuality with other religious scriptures, particularly the Torah and the Bible, is a testament to its integrative literary approach. The Quran frequently alludes to stories and characters from Jewish and Christian traditions, reinterpreting them within an Islamic framework. This intertextuality serves to establish a theological continuity and assert the Quran's position within the broader Abrahamic tradition.

For example, the Quranic account of the creation of Adam and the subsequent fall mirrors the biblical narrative in Genesis. Surah 2:30-39 details the creation of Adam, the command to the angels to prostrate before him, and the temptation by Iblis, paralleling the Genesis story while emphasizing unique Islamic theological perspectives.

Conclusion

The Quran's literary craftsmanship is a remarkable confluence of poetic tradition, divine inspiration, and meticulous human effort. Its integration of pre-Islamic poetic elements, combined with its theological profundity, underscores its position as a seminal text in Islamic and world literature. The interplay between divine and human agency in its revelation and compilation further enriches our understanding of its formation.

This chapter highlights the multifaceted nature of the Quran, inviting a deeper appreciation of its linguistic and literary sophistication. By acknowledging the contributions of pre-Islamic poetry, the role of Muhammad's companions, and the intertextual connections with earlier scriptures, one gains a more nuanced understanding of the Quran's unique and enduring legacy.

References:

1. Quran 2:23 - The challenge of producing a surah like the Quran.
2. Quran 99:1-8 - The depiction of the Day of Judgment.
3. Sahih Bukhari, Book 61, Hadith 509 - Muhammad instructing his scribes.
4. Sahih Bukhari, Book 61, Hadith 510 - Uthman's directive to compile the Quran.
5. Quran 2:30-39 - The creation of Adam narrative.

The Compilation and Preservation of the Quran

The Initial Compilation Efforts

The process of compiling the Quran into a single, cohesive text is a pivotal chapter in Islamic history. Following the death of the Prophet Muhammad, the need to preserve the Quranic revelations in a written form became paramount. This necessity was driven by the deaths of many who had memorized the Quran (Hafiz) during the Battle of Yamama, risking the loss of significant portions of the text.

The first caliph, Abu Bakr, heeded the advice of Umar ibn al-Khattab and commissioned Zayd ibn Thabit, a prominent scribe and close companion of the Prophet, to collect the Quranic verses. This effort is documented in Sahih Bukhari: "Abu Bakr said to me, 'You should search for the fragmentary scripts of the Quran and collect it in one book.' By Allah, if they had ordered me to move one of the mountains, it would not have been heavier for me than this ordering me to collect the Quran" (Sahih Bukhari, Book 66, Hadith 509).

The Role of Zayd ibn Thabit

Zayd ibn Thabit played a crucial role in the compilation process. He meticulously gathered the Quranic verses from various sources, including parchment, palm leaves, bones, and the memories of those who had memorized the Quran. His methodical approach ensured the accuracy and integrity of the text. Zayd's dedication is evident in his statement: "So I started looking for the Quran and collecting it from what was written on palm stalks, thin white stones, and also from the men who knew it by heart" (Sahih Bukhari, Book 66, Hadith 509).

Uthman's Standardization of the Quran

The standardization of the Quranic text was a significant milestone achieved during the caliphate of Uthman ibn Affan. As Islam expanded into diverse regions, variations in recitation and dialect posed a risk to the uniformity of the Quranic text. To address this, Uthman commissioned a committee, again led by Zayd ibn Thabit, to produce a standardized version of the Quran. Multiple copies of this standardized text were then distributed to major Islamic centers, and other versions were ordered to be destroyed to prevent discrepancies.

This initiative is chronicled in Sahih Bukhari: "Uthman sent to every Muslim province one copy of what they had copied, and ordered that all the other Quranic materials, whether written in fragmentary manuscripts or whole copies, be burnt" (Sahih Bukhari, Book 66, Hadith 510). This decisive action by Uthman ensured the preservation of the Quran in a consistent form across the expanding Islamic empire.

The Role of Oral Tradition

The oral tradition played a pivotal role in the preservation of the Quran. The Prophet Muhammad himself encouraged the memorization of the Quran, and many of his companions dedicated themselves to this task. The practice of oral transmission ensured that the Quranic text was preserved with remarkable accuracy, as reciters (Qurra) meticulously maintained the integrity of the verses.

The emphasis on oral transmission is reflected in numerous Hadiths. In one narration, the Prophet said, "The best among you are those who learn the Quran and teach it" (Sahih Bukhari, Book 61, Hadith 545). This tradition underscored the importance of both memorization and teaching, ensuring that the Quran would be preserved through successive generations.

The Role of Written Manuscripts

In addition to oral transmission, written manuscripts played a crucial role in the preservation of the Quran. The early Muslims utilized various materials, including parchment, leather, and papyrus, to document the Quranic verses. These manuscripts were meticulously copied and cross-checked for accuracy, contributing to the preservation of the text in its original form.

The Hadith literature underscores the importance of written documentation. In Sahih Muslim, it is recorded that the Prophet instructed, "Do not write down anything from me except the Quran. Whoever writes anything other than the Quran, let him erase it" (Sahih Muslim). This directive emphasized the need to preserve the Quranic text without any alterations or additions.

Modern Preservation and Study

The preservation of the Quran has continued into the modern era, with advancements in printing technology and digital media ensuring its widespread availability and accuracy. The use of printed copies, audio recordings, and digital platforms has facilitated the study and memorization of the Quran on an unprecedented scale.

Contemporary scholars continue to engage in the critical study of the Quran, utilizing historical manuscripts and modern technological tools to ensure the text's authenticity. Institutions dedicated to Quranic studies and the preservation of manuscripts play a vital role in maintaining the integrity of the Quranic text.

Conclusion

The compilation and preservation of the Quran represent a remarkable achievement in Islamic history, reflecting the dedication and meticulous efforts of the early Muslim community. The combined efforts of oral tradition, written manuscripts, and the standardization initiatives led by Uthman ibn Affan have ensured that the Quran remains preserved in its original form. This legacy continues to inspire and guide Muslims worldwide, underscoring the Quran's timeless significance as the divine word of Allah.

References:

1. Sahih Bukhari, Book 66, Hadith 509 - Compilation of the Quran by Zayd ibn Thabit.
2. Sahih Bukhari, Book 66, Hadith 510 - Uthman's standardization of the Quran.
3. Sahih Bukhari, Book 61, Hadith 545 - The importance of learning and teaching the Quran.
4. Sahih Muslim - Preservation of the Quranic text through written documentation.

CHAPTER 6
The Sociopolitical Context of Quranic Revelation

The Meccan Period: Struggle and Persecution

The early Meccan period of Muhammad's prophetic mission was marked by intense struggle and persecution. The socio-political environment in Mecca was dominated by the Quraysh tribe, whose leaders viewed Muhammad's monotheistic teachings as a direct threat to their economic and religious hegemony. The Quranic revelations during this period reflect a tone of resilience, patience, and steadfastness amidst adversity.

The Quran captures the essence of this struggle in several verses. For instance, Surah 73:10 advises patience in the face of insults: "And be patient over what they say and avoid them with gracious avoidance." This verse underscores the importance of maintaining composure and dignity despite the hostility encountered by Muhammad and his followers.

The Hadith literature also documents the hardships faced by early Muslims. In Sahih Bukhari (Book 58, Hadith 167), it is narrated that the companions of Muhammad endured severe persecution, including physical torture and social ostracism. These narratives highlight the profound sacrifices made by the early Muslim community in upholding their faith.

The Hijra: A Turning Point

The Hijra (migration) to Medina in 622 CE marked a pivotal turning point in the Islamic movement. This event not only provided a refuge for the beleaguered Muslim community but also laid the foundation for the establishment of an Islamic state. The Quranic revelations from the Medinan period reflect a shift in focus from individual endurance to the construction of a cohesive and just society.

Surah 2:218 encapsulates the significance of the Hijra: "Indeed, those who have believed and those who have emigrated and fought in the cause of Allah - those expect the mercy of Allah. And Allah is Forgiving and Merciful." This verse acknowledges the profound sacrifices involved in the migration and reinforces the promise of divine reward for those who undertook this arduous journey.

The Hadith further elaborates on the implications of the Hijra. In Sahih Muslim (Book 20, Hadith 4595), Muhammad is reported to have said, "Migration will not end until repentance ends, and repentance will not end until the sun rises from the west." This statement underscores the enduring significance of the Hijra as a symbol of faith and commitment to the Islamic cause.

The Medinan Period: Governance and Legislation

The Medinan period of Muhammad's life was characterized by the establishment of a nascent Islamic state and the implementation of comprehensive socio-political and legal reforms. The Quranic revelations during this period provided detailed guidance on various aspects of governance, community relations, and ethical conduct.

One of the key legislative milestones was the drafting of the Constitution of Medina, which outlined the rights and responsibilities of the Muslim and non-Muslim inhabitants of the city. This document is considered one of the earliest examples of a written constitution, emphasizing principles of justice, mutual protection, and communal harmony.

Surah 3:103 highlights the importance of unity and solidarity: "And hold firmly to the rope of Allah all together and do not become divided." This verse calls for communal cohesion and collective adherence to Islamic principles, serving as a foundational guideline for the governance of the diverse Medinan society.

The Conduct of War and Peace

The Quranic guidance on the conduct of war and peace reflects a balanced approach, emphasizing the principles of justice, restraint, and mercy. The revelations address the ethical dimensions of conflict, delineating the conditions under which war is permissible and the manner in which it should be conducted.

Surah 2:190 states, "Fight in the way of Allah those who fight you but do not transgress. Indeed. Allah does not like transgressors." This verse establishes the principle of proportionality and prohibits acts of aggression, underscoring the ethical constraints on warfare in Islamic jurisprudence.

The Hadith literature complements these guidelines by providing specific instructions on the treatment of prisoners and non-combatants. In Sahih Muslim (Book 19, Hadith 4319), Muhammad is reported to have instructed his followers to treat prisoners of war with kindness and to avoid harming women, children, and religious clergy. These teachings reflect a commitment to humanitarian principles even in the context of armed conflict.

The Role of Women and Social Reforms

The Quranic revelations also addressed the status and rights of women, introducing significant social reforms aimed at improving their position within the society. The revelations advocated for gender equity, emphasizing the spiritual and moral equality of men and women while recognizing their distinct roles and responsibilities.

Surah 4:1 underscores the equality and shared origin of all human beings: "O mankind, fear your Lord, who created you from one soul and created from it its mate and dispersed from both of them many men and women." This verse highlights the fundamental unity and equality of men and women, serving as a basis for the Quranic injunctions related to gender relations.

The Hadith further elaborates on the rights and responsibilities of women in various aspects of life, including marriage, inheritance, and education. In Sahih Bukhari (Book 3, Hadith 76), Muhammad is reported to have said, "Seeking knowledge is an obligation upon every Muslim." This statement underscores the importance of education for both men and women, reflecting the Quranic emphasis on the pursuit of knowledge and personal development.

Conclusion

The socio-political context of the Quranic revelation is integral to understanding the multifaceted nature of the Islamic message. The evolution from the Meccan period of persecution to the establishment of a just and cohesive society in Medina illustrates the dynamic interplay between religious principles and socio-political realities. The Quranic guidance on governance, conflict, and social reforms reflects a comprehensive approach to building a moral and just society, grounded in the principles of unity, justice, and compassion.

By examining the historical and socio-political dimensions of the Quranic revelation, one gains a deeper appreciation of its enduring relevance and the profound impact it has had on shaping the ethical and legal foundations of Islamic civilization.

References:

1. Quran 73:10 - Patience amidst persecution.
2. Sahih Bukhari, Book 58, Hadith 167 - Persecution of early Muslims.

3. Quran 2:218 - Significance of the Hijra.

4. Sahih Muslim, Book 20, Hadith 4595 - Enduring significance of the Hijra.

5. Quran 3:103 - Importance of unity and solidarity.

6. Surah 2:190 - Ethical constraints on warfare.

7. Sahih Muslim, Book 19, Hadith 4319 - Treatment of prisoners of war.

8. Quran 4:1 - Equality and shared origin of human beings.

9. Sahih Bukhari, Book 3, Hadith 76 - Obligation of seeking knowledge.

CHAPTER 7

The Quranic Perspective on Justice and Morality

Comprehensive Legal and Ethical Guidance

The Quranic framework for legal and ethical conduct is meticulously constructed, offering comprehensive guidance that encompasses various aspects of personal, social, and communal life. The Quran, alongside the Hadith, forms the bedrock of Sharia (Islamic law), which integrates divine directives with practical regulations to foster a just and harmonious society.

Surah 5:48 encapsulates this holistic approach: "And We have revealed to you, [O Muhammad], the Book in truth, confirming that which preceded it of the Scripture and as a criterion over it. So judge between them by what Allah has revealed and do not follow their inclinations away from what has come to you of the truth." This verse underscores the Quran's role as a definitive guide that validates and transcends previous scriptures, providing a comprehensive criterion for judgment.

Personal Conduct and Spiritual Development

The Quran emphasizes personal conduct and spiritual development as foundational elements of Islamic life. It advocates for a balanced approach that integrates ethical behavior with spiritual growth, ensuring that individuals cultivate virtues such as honesty, humility, patience, and compassion.

Surah 17:23-24 advises: "And your Lord has decreed that you not worship except Him, and to parents, good treatment. Whether one or both of them reach old age [while] with you, say not to them [so much as], 'uff,' and do not repel them but speak to them a noble word. And lower to them the wing of humility out of mercy and say, 'My Lord, have mercy upon them as they brought me up [when I was] small.'" This passage highlights the importance of filial piety and compassion, reflecting the broader ethical imperatives of Islam.

The Hadith literature reinforces these ethical teachings. In Sahih Muslim (Book 45, Hadith 100), the Prophet Muhammad states, "The best among you are those who have the best manners and character." This Hadith underscores the intrinsic value placed on good character and ethical conduct in Islam.

Social Justice and Community Welfare

The Quran's legal framework places significant emphasis on social justice and community welfare, mandating the equitable distribution of resources and the protection of the rights of the marginalized and vulnerable. The institution of Zakat (almsgiving) is a central mechanism for achieving economic justice and social solidarity.

Surah 2:177 elucidates the principle of comprehensive righteousness: "Righteousness is not that you turn your faces toward the east or the west, but [true] righteousness is in one who believes in Allah, the Last Day, the Angels, the Book, and the Prophets and gives his wealth, in spite of love for it, to relatives, orphans, the needy, the traveler, those who ask [for help], and for freeing slaves; [and who] establishes prayer and gives Zakat; [those who] fulfill their promise when they promise; and [those who] are patient in poverty and hardship and during battle. Those are the ones who have been true, and it is those who are the righteous."

The Hadith literature complements these Quranic directives by emphasizing the ethical dimensions of social justice. In Sahih Bukhari (Book 24, Hadith 573), the Prophet Muhammad is reported to have said, "Each of you is a shepherd and each of you is responsible for his flock." This Hadith underscores the collective responsibility of individuals to ensure the well-being of their community.

Legal Principles and Judicial Conduct

The Quran provides detailed legal principles that govern various aspects of judicial conduct, including criminal justice, family law, and commercial transactions. These principles are designed to uphold justice, fairness, and due process, ensuring that all members of society are treated equitably.

Surah 4:135 mandates impartiality in judgment: "O you who have believed, be persistently standing firm in justice, witnesses for Allah, even if it be against yourselves or parents and relatives. Whether one is rich or poor, Allah is more worthy of both. So follow not [personal] inclination, lest you not be just. And if you distort [your testimony] or refuse [to give it], then indeed Allah is ever, with what you do, Acquainted."

The Hadith literature provides practical guidance on judicial conduct. In Sahih Muslim (Book 20, Hadith 4493), the Prophet Muhammad advises, "When two litigants sit before you, do not decide until you have heard the other in the same manner as you have heard the first, for it is more fitting that the truth will become clear to you." This Hadith highlights the importance of fairness and thoroughness in judicial proceedings.

Economic Transactions and Ethical Business Practices

The Quranic framework for economic transactions emphasizes ethical business practices, transparency, and the prohibition of exploitative behaviors such as usury (Riba) and fraud. These regulations are intended to promote economic justice and ensure the integrity of market transactions.

Surah 2:275 categorically prohibits usury: "Those who consume interest cannot stand [on the Day of Resurrection] except as one stands who is being beaten by Satan into insanity. That is because they say, 'Trade is [just] like interest.' But Allah has permitted trade and has forbidden interest." This verse delineates the ethical boundaries of economic activities, promoting fair and equitable trade practices.

The Hadith literature further elaborates on the ethical principles of commerce. In Sahih Muslim (Book 10, Hadith 3663), the Prophet Muhammad states, "The truthful and trustworthy merchant is with the prophets, the truthful, and the martyrs." This Hadith emphasizes the moral integrity required in business dealings, reflecting the Quranic ethos of honesty and trustworthiness.

Environmental Stewardship and Resource Conservation

The Quran advocates for environmental stewardship and the sustainable use of natural resources, emphasizing the interconnectedness of all creation and the human responsibility to preserve the environment. This ecological consciousness is integral to the Quranic vision of a balanced and harmonious existence.

Surah 6:141 advises against wastefulness: "And He it is who produces gardens trellised and untrellised, and date-palms, and crops of different shape and taste (its fruits and its seeds) and olives, and pomegranates, similar (in kind) and different (in taste). Eat of their fruit when they ripen, but pay the due thereof (its Zakat) on the day of its harvest, and waste not by extravagance. Verily, He likes not Al-Musrifun (those who waste by extravagance)."

The Hadith literature reinforces the principle of conservation. In Sunan Ibn Majah (Book 2, Hadith 425), the Prophet Muhammad is reported to have said, "The world is green and beautiful, and Allah has appointed you as His stewards over it. He sees how you acquit yourselves." This Hadith underscores the ethical mandate to protect and sustain the natural environment.

Conclusion

The Quranic framework for legal and ethical conduct is a comprehensive and integrative system that addresses various dimensions of human existence. Its emphasis on personal virtue, social justice, economic integrity, and environmental stewardship reflects a holistic approach to fostering a just and harmonious society. The Hadith literature enriches this framework by providing practical examples and detailed expositions of the Quranic principles, ensuring their effective implementation in daily life. Together, the Quran and Hadith offer a timeless and profound guide for ethical and moral conduct, underscoring the enduring relevance and universality of Islamic teachings.

References:

1. Surah 5:48 - The Quran as a definitive guide and criterion.
2. Surah 17:23-24 - Importance of filial piety and compassion.
3. Sahih Muslim, Book 45, Hadith 100 - Value of good character and ethical conduct.
4. Surah 2:177 - Comprehensive righteousness.
5. Sahih Bukhari, Book 24, Hadith 573 - Collective responsibility for community welfare.
6. Surah 4:135 - Impartiality in judgment.
7. Sahih Muslim, Book 20, Hadith 4493 - Fairness in judicial proceedings.
8. Surah 2:275 - Prohibition of usury.
9. Sahih Muslim, Book 10, Hadith 3663 - Moral integrity in business dealings.
10. Surah 6:141 - Against wastefulness and extravagance.

11. Sunan Ibn Majah, Book 2, Hadith 425 - Environmental stewardship and conservation.

CHAPTER 8
The Eschatological Vision in the Quran

The Concept of the Afterlife

The Quran presents a vivid and compelling eschatological vision, delineating a clear and detailed concept of the afterlife. This vision encompasses the Day of Judgment (Yawm al-Qiyamah), resurrection, heaven (Jannah), and hell (Jahannam). The Quranic depiction of the afterlife serves not only as a theological tenet but also as a moral impetus, urging believers to lead righteous lives in anticipation of divine accountability.

Surah 75:3-4 states, "Does man think that We will not assemble his bones? Yes. We are Able to [even] proportion his fingertips." This verse underscores the Quranic assertion of bodily resurrection, emphasizing God's omnipotence and the inevitability of the resurrection.

The Day of Judgment

The Day of Judgment is a central theme in the Quranic eschatology, portrayed with dramatic and awe-inspiring imagery. It is depicted as a time of ultimate reckoning, where every soul will be held accountable for its deeds. The Quran describes the signs of the Last Day, the resurrection of the dead, and the final judgment with profound detail.

In Surah 99:1-8 (Al-Zalzalah), the Quran states, "When the earth is shaken with its [final] earthquake and the earth discharges its burdens, and man says, 'What is [wrong] with it?' That Day, it will report its news because your Lord has commanded it. That Day, the people will depart separated [into categories] to be shown [the result of] their deeds. So whoever does an atom's weight of good will see it, and whoever does an atom's weight of evil will see it." This passage vividly depicts the apocalyptic upheaval and the ensuing judgment, reinforcing the Quranic emphasis on individual accountability.

Heaven and Hell

The Quran provides elaborate descriptions of heaven and hell, contrasting the eternal bliss of the righteous with the perpetual torment of the wicked. These depictions serve as powerful incentives for moral and ethical conduct, highlighting the ultimate consequences of one's actions.

Heaven (Jannah) is portrayed as a place of unparalleled beauty and pleasure, reserved for those who have lived righteously and faithfully. Surah 55:46-48 states, "But for he who has feared the position of his Lord are two gardens. So which of the favors of your Lord would you deny? Having [spreading] branches." This depiction of paradise emphasizes both its physical and spiritual delights, offering a vision of eternal reward for the virtuous.

In contrast, hell (Jahannam) is described in terms of severe punishment and relentless suffering. Surah 4:56 warns, "Indeed, those who disbelieve in Our verses - We will drive them into a Fire. Every time their skins are roasted through We will replace them with other skins so they may taste the punishment. Indeed, Allah is ever Exalted in Might and Wise." This harrowing portrayal serves as a deterrent against disbelief and sinful behavior.

The Intermediary State (Barzakh)

The concept of Barzakh, the intermediary state between death and resurrection, is also addressed in the Quran. This state serves as a transitional period where souls await the final judgment. The Quran alludes to this state in Surah 23:99-100, stating, "Until, when death comes to one of them, he says, 'My Lord, send me back that I might do righteousness in that which I left behind.' No! It is only a word he is saying; and behind them is a barrier until the Day they are resurrected."

The Hadith literature further elucidates the nature of Barzakh, providing insights into the experiences of the soul during this period. In Sahih Muslim (Book 40, Hadith 6862), it is narrated that the Prophet Muhammad described the questioning of the soul by angels in the grave, emphasizing the continuation of moral responsibility even after death.

The Role of Intercession

Intercession (Shafa'ah) plays a significant role in the Quranic eschatological framework. It refers to the act of pleading on behalf of others, particularly on the Day of Judgment. The Quran acknowledges the possibility of intercession but emphasizes that it is ultimately subject to Allah's will.

Surah 2:255 (Ayat al-Kursi) states, "Who is it that can intercede with Him except by His permission?" This verse highlights the conditional nature of intercession, underscoring that it is granted solely by divine consent.

The Hadith literature provides further context on intercession, with numerous traditions describing the intercessory role of the Prophet Muhammad. In Sahih Bukhari (Book 76, Hadith 570), it is reported that the Prophet said, "My intercession will be for those of my nation who committed major sins." This Hadith illustrates the merciful aspect of intercession, offering hope for those who have erred but remain within the fold of Islam.

The Moral and Ethical Implications

The Quranic eschatological vision has profound moral and ethical implications. It serves as a constant reminder of the transient nature of worldly life and the enduring significance of one's actions. By emphasizing the certainty of the afterlife and the final judgment, the Quran encourages believers to lead lives of piety, integrity, and social responsibility.

Surah 57:20 reinforces this perspective: "Know that the life of this world is but amusement and diversion and adornment and boasting to one another and competition in increase of wealth and children. Like the example of a rain whose [resulting] plant growth pleases the tillers; then it dries and you see it turned yellow; then it becomes [scattered] debris. And in the Hereafter is severe punishment and forgiveness from Allah and approval. And what is the worldly life except the enjoyment of delusion." This verse encapsulates the Quranic view of worldly life as ephemeral and ultimately insignificant compared to the eternal hereafter.

Conclusion

The Quran's eschatological vision is a cornerstone of its theological and moral framework. It vividly portrays the realities of the afterlife, encompassing the Day of Judgment, resurrection, heaven, hell, and the intermediary state. These teachings serve to instill a profound sense of accountability and ethical consciousness among believers, urging them to strive for righteousness in anticipation of divine recompense.

By exploring the rich eschatological themes in the Quran and Hadith, one gains a deeper understanding of the Islamic worldview and its emphasis on the ultimate justice and mercy of Allah. This eschatological perspective not only shapes individual behavior but also underpins the broader moral and ethical ethos of the Muslim community.

References:

1. Quran 75:3-4 - Assembling of bones and bodily resurrection.

2. Quran 99:1-8 - Day of Judgment and individual accountability.

3. Surah 55:46-48 - Description of heaven.

4. Surah 4:56 - Description of hell.

5. Surah 23:99-100 - Concept of Barzakh.

6. Sahih Muslim, Book 40, Hadith 6862 - Questioning of the soul in the grave.

7. Surah 2:255 - Conditional nature of intercession.

8. Sahih Bukhari, Book 76, Hadith 570 - Intercessory role of the Prophet Muhammad.

9. Surah 57:20 - Transient nature of worldly life.

C H A P T E R 9

The Quran's Influence on Legal Ethical Systems

The Foundation of Sharia

The Quran serves as the primary source of Islamic law, known as Sharia, which encompasses a comprehensive legal and ethical system governing various aspects of individual and communal life. Sharia derives its principles from the Quranic text, which provides explicit directives on matters such as worship, family relations, commerce, and criminal justice. These principles are further elaborated through the Hadith, the recorded sayings and actions of the Prophet Muhammad, offering practical guidance on the implementation of Quranic injunctions.

Surah 5:48 articulates the Quran's role as a legal and ethical guide: "And We have sent down to you the Book in truth, confirming that which preceded it of the Scripture and as a criterion over it. So judge between them by what Allah has revealed and do not follow their inclinations away from what has come to you of the truth." This verse underscores the Quran's authority in adjudicating legal matters and its role as the ultimate arbiter of truth and justice.

The Role of the Hadith in Sharia

The Hadith literature complements the Quran by providing detailed expositions and practical applications of its teachings. These traditions elucidate various aspects of Islamic jurisprudence, from ritual practices to social ethics, thereby enriching the Quranic legal framework. The synthesis of the Quran and Hadith forms the bedrock of Sharia, guiding Muslims in their daily lives and communal interactions.

For instance, in Sahih Bukhari (Book 52, Hadith 43), the Prophet Muhammad is reported to have said, "The most beloved places to Allah are the mosques, and the most hated places to Allah are the markets." This Hadith highlights the ethical considerations in economic transactions, emphasizing the importance of integrity and piety over material pursuits.

Family Law and Gender Relations

The Quran provides comprehensive guidance on family law, including marriage, divorce, inheritance, and child custody. These laws aim to promote justice, balance, and compassion within the family unit, ensuring the protection of rights for all members, particularly women and children.

Surah 4:1 emphasizes the equality and shared origin of all human beings: "O mankind, fear your Lord, who created you from one soul and created from it its mate and dispersed from both of them many men and women." This verse serves as the foundation for the Quranic principles of gender equity and mutual respect in familial relationships.

The Hadith further elaborates on the responsibilities and rights of spouses. In Sahih Muslim (Book 8, Hadith 3467), it is narrated that the Prophet said, "The best of you are those who are best to their wives." This Hadith underscores the importance of kindness and equitable treatment within marriage, reflecting the Quranic ethos of compassion and justice.

Economic Justice and Social Welfare

The Quranic injunctions on economic justice and social welfare form a crucial component of Sharia. These principles advocate for the equitable distribution of wealth, the prohibition of exploitative practices, and the provision of support for the needy and vulnerable.

Surah 2:275 condemns usury (Riba): "Those who consume interest cannot stand [on the Day of Resurrection] except as one stands who is being beaten by Satan into insanity. That is because they say, 'Trade is [just] like interest.' But Allah has permitted trade and has forbidden interest." This verse delineates the ethical boundaries of economic transactions, promoting fairness and integrity in financial dealings.

The institution of Zakat (almsgiving) is another cornerstone of Islamic economic justice. Surah 9:60 outlines the categories of recipients for Zakat: "Zakat expenditures are only for the poor and for the needy and for those employed to collect [Zakat] and for bringing hearts together [for Islam] and for freeing captives [or slaves] and for those in debt and for the cause of Allah and for the [stranded] traveler - an obligation [imposed] by Allah. And Allah is Knowing and Wise." This directive ensures the redistribution of wealth and the provision of social safety nets, fostering a sense of communal solidarity and responsibility.

Criminal Justice and Ethical Conduct

The Quranic approach to criminal justice emphasizes both deterrence and rehabilitation, aiming to uphold social order while ensuring fairness and mercy. The prescribed punishments for specific offenses are intended to serve as deterrents, while the overarching principles of justice and compassion guide their implementation.

Surah 5:38 prescribes the punishment for theft: "As for the thief, the male and the female, amputate their hands in recompense for what they committed as a deterrent [punishment] from Allah. And Allah is Exalted in Might and Wise." This verse underscores the severity of theft while also highlighting the need for proportionality and justice in its application.

The Hadith literature provides further insights into the administration of criminal justice. In Sahih Muslim (Book 17, Hadith 4191), the Prophet emphasized the importance of avoiding legal punishment in cases of doubt, stating, "Avert the legal punishments from the Muslims as much as possible, and if there is any way out, then let them go, for it is better for the ruler to err in forgiveness than to err in punishment." This teaching reflects the Quranic emphasis on mercy and the avoidance of unjust punishment.

Ethical Principles and Personal Conduct

The Quran's ethical principles extend beyond legal injunctions to encompass personal conduct and moral behavior. It advocates for virtues such as honesty, humility, patience, and generosity, urging believers to embody these qualities in their interactions with others.

Surah 3:134 highlights the virtues of forgiveness and restraint: "Who spend [in the cause of Allah] during ease and hardship and who restrain anger and who pardon the people - and Allah loves the doers of good." This verse encourages ethical conduct and the cultivation of a virtuous character, reflecting the Quran's holistic approach to morality.

The Hadith literature reinforces these ethical teachings, offering practical examples of virtuous behavior. In Sahih Bukhari (Book 8, Hadith 73), the Prophet Muhammad is reported to have said, "The most perfect of believers in faith are those who are best in their character." This Hadith underscores the integral connection between faith and ethical conduct, emphasizing the importance of moral excellence in the life of a believer.

Conclusion

The Quran's influence on legal and ethical systems is profound and far-reaching, shaping the foundational principles of Sharia and guiding the moral conduct of Muslims. Through its comprehensive legal framework and ethical teachings, the Quran seeks to establish a just and harmonious society, grounded in the principles of fairness, compassion, and accountability.

The Hadith literature further enriches this framework, providing detailed expositions and practical applications of Quranic injunctions. Together, the Quran and Hadith form a cohesive and dynamic system of guidance, addressing the complexities of human life and fostering a community committed to justice and moral integrity.

By exploring the Quran's legal and ethical dimensions, one gains a deeper appreciation of its enduring relevance and the transformative impact it has had on Islamic civilization and beyond.

References:

1. Surah 5:48 - Quran as a criterion and guide.
2. Sahih Bukhari, Book 52, Hadith 43 - Ethical considerations in economic transactions.
3. Surah 4:1 - Equality and shared origin of all human beings.
4. Sahih Muslim, Book 8, Hadith 3467 - Kindness to wives.
5. Surah 2:275 - Prohibition of usury.
6. Surah 9:60 - Categories of Zakat recipients.
7. Surah 5:38 - Punishment for theft.
8. Sahih Muslim, Book 17, Hadith 4191 - Avoiding unjust punishment.
9. Surah 3:134 - Virtues of forgiveness and restraint.
10. Sahih Bukhari, Book 8, Hadith 73 - Connection between faith and ethical conduct.

CHAPTER 10
The Quranic Concept of Knowledge and Education

The Primacy of Knowledge in the Quran

The Quran places immense emphasis on the pursuit of knowledge, considering it a fundamental aspect of faith and an essential virtue. Knowledge ('Ilm) in the Quranic context encompasses both religious and worldly sciences, promoting a holistic approach to education that nurtures intellectual, spiritual, and ethical development. The Quranic exhortation to seek knowledge is grounded in the belief that understanding the world and its phenomena leads to a deeper appreciation of the Creator's wisdom.

Surah 96:1-5, often cited as the first revelation received by Muhammad, underscores this emphasis: "Recite in the name of your Lord who created – Created man from a clinging substance. Recite, and your Lord is the most Generous – Who taught by the pen – Taught man that which he knew not." This passage highlights the divine imperative to seek knowledge and the transformative power of learning.

The Role of the Hadith in Promoting Education

The Hadith literature further reinforces the Quranic emphasis on knowledge, providing detailed accounts of the Prophet Muhammad's teachings and actions that encourage learning and intellectual growth. These traditions underscore the importance of education for both men and women, reflecting the inclusive nature of Islamic pedagogy.

In Sahih Muslim (Book 4, Hadith 1371), the Prophet Muhammad is reported to have said, "Seeking knowledge is an obligation upon every Muslim." This Hadith emphasizes the universal nature of the quest for knowledge, making it a religious duty for all believers.

The Integration of Religious and Secular Knowledge

The Quran advocates for the integration of religious and secular knowledge, encouraging believers to explore the natural world and its mysteries. This integrated approach to education is exemplified in numerous Quranic verses that call for reflection and inquiry into the natural phenomena as signs of Allah's creative power.

Surah 3:190-191 states, "Indeed, in the creation of the heavens and the earth and the alternation of the night and the day are signs for those of understanding – Who remember Allah while standing or sitting or [lying] on their sides and give thought to the creation of the heavens and the earth, [saying], 'Our Lord, You did not create this aimlessly; exalted are You [above such a thing]; then protect us from the punishment of the Fire.'" This passage encourages contemplation and intellectual engagement with the natural world as a means of strengthening faith.

The Establishment of Educational Institutions

The emphasis on knowledge and education in the Quran and Hadith laid the foundation for the establishment of numerous educational institutions throughout Islamic history. Madrasas, libraries, and centers of learning flourished in various parts of the Islamic world, contributing to advancements in science, medicine, philosophy, and the arts.

The establishment of the House of Wisdom (Bayt al-Hikmah) in Baghdad during the Abbasid Caliphate is a notable example. This institution became a major center for the translation and study of scientific and philosophical texts from various cultures, reflecting the Quranic spirit of intellectual curiosity and openness to diverse sources of knowledge.

The Ethical Dimensions of Knowledge

The Quranic concept of knowledge is inherently tied to ethical considerations. The pursuit of knowledge is not an end in itself but is intended to foster moral and spiritual growth. The Quran cautions against the misuse of knowledge and emphasizes the responsibility that comes with it.

Surah 2:269 highlights this ethical dimension: "He grants wisdom to whom He wills, and whoever has been granted wisdom has certainly been given much good. And none will remember except those of understanding." This verse associates wisdom with ethical discernment and the capacity to use knowledge for the greater good.

The Hadith literature also addresses the ethical implications of knowledge. In Sahih Bukhari (Book 3, Hadith 56), the Prophet Muhammad is reported to have said, "The best of you are those who learn the Quran and teach it." This Hadith underscores the importance of using knowledge to benefit others, reflecting the Quranic ethos of communal responsibility and ethical conduct.

The Impact of Quranic Teachings on Contemporary Education

The Quranic emphasis on knowledge and education continues to influence contemporary Muslim societies. Educational institutions, curricula, and pedagogical practices in many parts of the Islamic world are informed by Quranic principles and the Hadith. Efforts to revive and integrate traditional Islamic education with modern scientific and technological advancements are ongoing, reflecting the dynamic and evolving nature of Islamic scholarship.

In contemporary discourse, the Quranic call for the pursuit of knowledge is often invoked to address challenges in education, science, and technology. The holistic approach to education advocated by the Quran encourages a balanced development of intellectual, spiritual, and ethical faculties, aiming to produce well-rounded individuals capable of contributing positively to society.

Conclusion

The Quranic concept of knowledge and education is comprehensive and multifaceted, encompassing religious and secular learning while emphasizing ethical considerations. The Quran and Hadith together advocate for the pursuit of knowledge as a means of achieving intellectual, spiritual, and moral growth. This profound emphasis on education has historically inspired the establishment of significant centers of learning and continues to shape contemporary educational practices in the Muslim world.

By exploring the Quranic teachings on knowledge, one gains a deeper appreciation of the integral role of education in Islamic thought and its enduring relevance in fostering intellectual and moral development.

References:

1. Surah 96:1-5 - The imperative to seek knowledge.
2. Sahih Muslim, Book 4, Hadith 1371 - Obligation of seeking knowledge.
3. Surah 3:190-191 - Reflection on natural phenomena as signs of Allah.
4. Surah 2:269 - Ethical dimension of wisdom.
5. Sahih Bukhari, Book 3, Hadith 56 - The best of you are those who learn and teach the Quran.

CHAPTER 11

The Quranic Paradigm of Community and Social Responsibility

The Concept of Ummah

The Quranic paradigm of community, encapsulated in the term Ummah, represents a comprehensive vision of social cohesion, mutual responsibility, and collective identity. The term Ummah signifies a community bound together by shared faith, values, and ethical principles, transcending ethnic, racial, and national boundaries. This concept is central to the Quran's vision of a just and harmonious society, where individuals are expected to contribute to the common good and uphold collective welfare.

Surah 3:110 extols the virtues of the Muslim community: "You are the best nation produced [as an example] for mankind. You enjoin what is right and forbid what is wrong and believe in Allah." This verse underscores the communal responsibility to promote ethical conduct and uphold justice, reflecting the Quranic emphasis on social responsibility.

The Role of Brotherhood and Solidarity

Brotherhood and solidarity are fundamental to the Quranic vision of community. The Quran and Hadith emphasize the importance of mutual support, empathy, and cooperation among believers, fostering a sense of unity and collective strength.

Surah 49:10 states, "The believers are but brothers, so make settlement between your brothers. And fear Allah that you may receive mercy." This verse highlights the fraternal bonds that unite the Muslim community and the imperative to resolve conflicts and maintain harmony.

The Hadith literature reinforces this ethos of brotherhood. In Sahih Bukhari (Book 2, Hadith 13), the Prophet Muhammad is reported to have said, "None of you will believe until you love for your brother what you love for yourself." This Hadith encapsulates the principle of altruism and empathy, which is central to the Quranic vision of a cohesive community.

Social Justice and Welfare

The Quran places a strong emphasis on social justice and the welfare of the marginalized and vulnerable. It advocates for the equitable distribution of resources, the protection of rights, and the provision of support to those in need. This commitment to social justice is manifested in various Quranic injunctions and institutional mechanisms, such as Zakat (almsgiving) and Sadaqah (charitable giving).

Surah 4:36 instructs, "Worship Allah and associate nothing with Him, and to parents do good, and to relatives, orphans, the needy, the near neighbor, the neighbor farther away, the companion at your side, the traveler, and those whom your right hands possess. Indeed, Allah does not like those who are self-deluding and boastful." This verse underscores the comprehensive scope of social responsibility, encompassing family, neighbors, and the broader community.

The Hadith literature further elaborates on the importance of social welfare. In Sahih Muslim (Book 32, Hadith 6251), the Prophet Muhammad is reported to have said, "He is not a believer whose stomach is filled while his neighbor goes hungry." This Hadith highlights the moral imperative to ensure the welfare of others, reflecting the Quranic ethos of compassion and communal solidarity.

The Institution of Zakat and Charitable Giving

Zakat, one of the Five Pillars of Islam, is a key institution for promoting social welfare and economic justice. It mandates the redistribution of wealth to support the poor and needy, thereby fostering economic equity and reducing social disparities.

Surah 9:60 outlines the categories of Zakat recipients: "Zakat expenditures are only for the poor and for the needy and for those employed to collect [Zakat] and for bringing hearts together [for Islam] and for freeing captives [or slaves] and for those in debt and for the cause of Allah and for the [stranded] traveler - an obligation [imposed] by Allah. And Allah is Knowing and Wise." This directive ensures that Zakat serves as a comprehensive social safety net, addressing various aspects of socio-economic deprivation.

Sadaqah, or voluntary charitable giving, complements Zakat by encouraging additional acts of generosity and support for the less fortunate. The Quran extols the virtues of Sadaqah in Surah 2:261: "The example of those who spend their wealth in the way of Allah is like a seed [of grain] that sprouts seven ears; in every ear are a hundred grains. And Allah multiplies [His reward] for whom He wills. And Allah is all-Encompassing and Knowing." This verse highlights the spiritual and communal benefits of charitable giving, promoting a culture of generosity and mutual aid.

The Ethical Framework of Community Conduct

The Quran provides a comprehensive ethical framework for community conduct, emphasizing values such as honesty, justice, and mutual respect. These ethical principles are designed to foster trust and cooperation within the community, ensuring that social interactions are conducted with integrity and fairness.

Surah 5:8 instructs, "O you who have believed, be persistently standing firm for Allah, witnesses in justice, and do not let the hatred of a people prevent you from being just. Be just; that is nearer to righteousness. And fear Allah; indeed, Allah is Acquainted with what you do." This verse underscores the imperative of justice and impartiality, even in the face of personal biases and enmities.

The Hadith literature provides practical guidance on ethical conduct. In Sahih Bukhari (Book 78, Hadith 611), the Prophet Muhammad is reported to have said, "The signs of a hypocrite are three: when he speaks, he lies; when he makes a promise, he breaks it; and when he is entrusted with something, he betrays that trust." This Hadith highlights the importance of truthfulness, reliability, and trustworthiness, which are essential for maintaining social cohesion and mutual trust.

The Role of Women in Community Life

The Quran acknowledges the vital role of women in community life, advocating for their rights and responsibilities within the family and society. It emphasizes gender equity and the importance of mutual respect and cooperation between men and women.

Surah 33:35 states, "Indeed, the Muslim men and Muslim women, the believing men and believing women, the obedient men and obedient women, the truthful men and truthful women, the patient men and patient women, the humble men and humble women, the charitable men and charitable women, the fasting men and fasting women, the men who guard their private parts and the women who do so, and the men who remember Allah often and the women who do so - for them Allah has prepared forgiveness and a great reward." This verse highlights the equal spiritual and moral status of men and women, reflecting the Quranic vision of a just and inclusive community.

The Hadith literature also emphasizes the active participation of women in community affairs. In Sahih Bukhari (Book 62, Hadith 135), it is narrated that the Prophet Muhammad consulted his wife, Umm Salamah, during the Treaty of Hudaybiyyah, illustrating the importance of women's counsel and involvement in decision-making processes.

Conclusion

The Quranic paradigm of community and social responsibility is comprehensive and multifaceted, encompassing principles of justice, solidarity, and mutual respect. It emphasizes the collective identity and shared responsibilities of the Ummah, promoting social cohesion and ethical conduct. The Hadith literature enriches this paradigm, offering practical guidance on community interactions and the fulfillment of social obligations.

By exploring the Quranic teachings on community and social responsibility, one gains a deeper appreciation of the ethical and moral foundations of Islamic society. This paradigm encourages believers to actively contribute to the welfare of their community, fostering a just and harmonious social order.

References:

1. Surah 3:110 - The virtues of the Muslim community.
2. Surah 49:10 - Brotherhood among believers.
3. Sahih Bukhari, Book 2, Hadith 13 - Loving for one's brother what one loves for oneself.
4. Surah 4:36 - Comprehensive scope of social responsibility.
5. Sahih Muslim, Book 32, Hadith 6251 - Moral imperative of ensuring the welfare of others.
6. Surah 9:60 - Categories of Zakat recipients.
7. Surah 2:261 - Virtues of charitable giving.

8. Surah 5:8 - Imperative of justice and impartiality.

9. Sahih Bukhari, Book 78, Hadith 611 - Signs of a hypocrite.

10. Surah 33:35 - Equal spiritual and moral status of men and women.

11. Sahih Bukhari, Book 62, Hadith 135 - Importance of women's counsel in decision-making.

CHAPTER 12
The Quranic Vision of Leadership and Governance

The Concept of Leadership in Islam

The Quran delineates a comprehensive framework for leadership and governance, emphasizing principles of justice, consultation (Shura), and accountability. Leadership in Islam is viewed not merely as a position of authority but as a trust (Amanah) and a profound responsibility bestowed by Allah. This Quranic vision aims to establish a just and moral society, where leaders are accountable to both Allah and their constituents.

Surah 4:58 underscores the ethical imperative of leadership: "Indeed, Allah commands you to render trusts to whom they are due and when you judge between people to judge with justice. Excellent is that which Allah instructs you. Indeed, Allah is ever Hearing and Seeing." This verse highlights the fundamental principles of trust and justice that underpin Islamic leadership.

The Role of Consultation (Shura)

Consultation (Shura) is a pivotal concept in the Quranic vision of governance, advocating for collective decision-making and inclusive leadership. The practice of Shura ensures that leaders consider the perspectives and welfare of their community, fostering a participatory and transparent governance system.

Surah 42:38 extols the virtues of Shura: "And those who have responded to their lord and established prayer and whose affair is [determined by] consultation among themselves, and from what We have provided them, they spend." This verse enshrines consultation as a fundamental aspect of community affairs, promoting a governance model rooted in mutual respect and collective wisdom.

The Hadith literature reinforces the importance of Shura in leadership. In Sahih Bukhari (Book 92, Hadith 30), it is narrated that the Prophet Muhammad frequently consulted his companions on various matters, exemplifying the Quranic principle of inclusive decision-making.

Justice as a Pillar of Governance

Justice (Adl) is a cornerstone of the Quranic framework for leadership and governance. The Quran repeatedly emphasizes the obligation of leaders to uphold justice, protect the rights of individuals, and ensure equitable treatment for all members of society. This commitment to justice is seen as integral to the legitimacy and effectiveness of leadership.

Surah 5:8 instructs, "O you who have believed, be persistently standing firm for Allah, witnesses in justice, and do not let the hatred of a people prevent you from being just. Be just; that is nearer to righteousness. And fear Allah; indeed, Allah is Acquainted with what you do." This verse underscores the imperative of impartiality and justice, even in the face of personal enmities.

The Hadith further elaborates on the principles of justice in governance. In Sahih Muslim (Book 20, Hadith 4546), the Prophet Muhammad is reported to have said, "There is no governor who oppresses the people under his rule but Allah will make him suffer the torment of Hell." This Hadith highlights the severe accountability faced by unjust leaders, reinforcing the Quranic mandate for justice.

Accountability and Ethical Conduct

The Quranic vision of leadership is deeply intertwined with the concepts of accountability and ethical conduct. Leaders are seen as stewards who will be held accountable by Allah for their actions and decisions. This accountability extends to both their governance and their personal conduct, underscoring the moral and ethical responsibilities of leadership.

Surah 3:161 cautions against betrayal of trust: "It is not attributable to any prophet that he would act unfaithfully [in regard to war booty]. And whoever betrays, [taking unlawfully], will come with what he took on the Day of Resurrection. Then will every soul be [fully] compensated for what it earned, and they will not be wronged." This verse highlights the severe consequences of betrayal and emphasizes the ethical integrity expected of leaders.

The Hadith literature also addresses the importance of accountability. In Sahih Bukhari (Book 24, Hadith 573), the Prophet Muhammad is reported to have said, "Each of you is a shepherd and each of you is responsible for his flock." This Hadith reinforces the notion of accountability, emphasizing the responsibility of leaders to their community.

The Ideal Qualities of a Leader

The Quran and Hadith outline the ideal qualities and characteristics of a leader, emphasizing virtues such as wisdom, humility, courage, and piety. These qualities are essential for effective and ethical leadership, enabling leaders to guide their communities with justice and compassion.

Surah 2:247 describes the qualities of a divinely chosen leader: "And their prophet said to them, 'Indeed, Allah has sent to you Saul as a king.' They said, 'How can he have kingship over us while we are more worthy of kingship than him and he has not been given any measure of wealth?' He said, 'Indeed, Allah has chosen him over you and has increased him abundantly in knowledge and stature. And Allah gives His sovereignty to whom He wills. And Allah is all-Encompassing [in favor] and Knowing.'" This verse highlights the divine criteria for leadership, prioritizing knowledge and moral stature over material wealth.

The Hadith literature provides additional insights into the qualities of a leader. In Sahih Muslim (Book 20, Hadith 4493), the Prophet Muhammad is reported to have said, "The best of your leaders are those whom you love and who love you, who pray for you and you pray for them." This Hadith underscores the importance of mutual affection and support between leaders and their communities, reflecting the ethical and compassionate nature of ideal leadership.

The Practical Implementation of Quranic Governance

The practical implementation of Quranic principles of governance has historically varied, reflecting the diverse socio-political contexts of Muslim societies. However, the core principles of justice, consultation, accountability, and ethical conduct remain central to Islamic governance, providing a foundational framework that guides contemporary political thought and practice in the Muslim world.

In modern times, efforts to integrate Quranic principles with democratic governance models have been explored, aiming to reconcile traditional Islamic values with contemporary political realities. These efforts reflect the enduring relevance of the Quranic vision of leadership and governance, emphasizing its adaptability and applicability across different historical and cultural contexts.

Conclusion

The Quranic vision of leadership and governance is a comprehensive and ethically grounded framework that emphasizes justice, consultation, accountability, and ethical conduct. This paradigm seeks to establish a just and moral society, where leaders are entrusted with the responsibility to serve their communities with integrity and compassion. The Hadith literature further enriches this framework, providing practical guidance and reinforcing the ethical principles outlined in the Quran.

By exploring the Quranic teachings on leadership and governance, one gains a deeper appreciation of the moral and ethical foundations of Islamic political thought. This vision continues to inspire contemporary efforts to create just and equitable governance systems, reflecting the timeless relevance of the Quranic principles in shaping a harmonious and ethical society.

References:

1. Surah 4:58 - Ethical imperative of leadership.
2. Surah 42:38 - Virtues of consultation.
3. Sahih Bukhari, Book 92, Hadith 30 - Prophet Muhammad's consultation with companions.
4. Surah 5:8 - Imperative of justice and impartiality.
5. Sahih Muslim, Book 20, Hadith 4546 - Accountability for unjust leaders.
6. Surah 3:161 - Consequences of betrayal of trust.
7. Sahih Bukhari, Book 24, Hadith 573 - Accountability of leaders.
8. Surah 2:247 - Qualities of a divinely chosen leader.
9. Sahih Muslim, Book 20, Hadith 4493 - Mutual affection between leaders and communities.

CHAPTER 13

The Quranic Vision of Environmental Stewardship

The Concept of Stewardship (Khilafah)

The Quran espouses a profound vision of environmental stewardship, rooted in the concept of Khilafah (stewardship). Human beings are considered stewards of the Earth, entrusted with its care and preservation. This responsibility is a divine mandate, emphasizing the interconnectedness of all creation and the moral duty to maintain the balance (Mizan) that Allah has established.

Surah 6:165 elucidates this role: "And it is He who has made you successors upon the earth and has raised some of you above others in degrees [of rank] that He may try you through what He has given you. Indeed, your Lord is swift in penalty; but indeed, He is Forgiving and Merciful." This verse highlights the stewardship role of humanity and the accountability that accompanies it.

The Principle of Balance (Mizan)

The principle of balance (Mizan) is central to the Quranic vision of environmental stewardship. It underscores the need to maintain harmony within the natural world, avoiding excess and exploitation. The Quran teaches that all creation is meticulously balanced and that human actions should reflect this divine equilibrium.

Surah 55:7-9 states, "And the heaven He raised and imposed the balance that you not transgress within the balance. And establish weight in justice and do not make deficient the balance." These verses call for adherence to the natural balance, promoting sustainable and equitable use of resources.

The Hadith literature also reinforces this principle. In Sahih Bukhari (Book 72, Hadith 843), the Prophet Muhammad is reported to have said, "The world is green and beautiful, and Allah has appointed you as His stewards over it. He sees how you acquit yourselves." This Hadith emphasizes the beauty and fragility of the natural world and the responsibility of humans to protect it.

Conservation of Resources

The Quran advocates for the conservation of resources, discouraging wastefulness and encouraging mindful consumption. The concept of conservation is integral to Islamic environmental ethics, reflecting a deep respect for the finite nature of the Earth's resources.

Surah 7:31 instructs, "O children of Adam, take your adornment at every masjid, and eat and drink, but be not excessive. Indeed, He likes not those who commit excess." This verse promotes moderation and warns against the detrimental effects of extravagance.

The Hadith literature provides further guidance on resource conservation. In Sahih Muslim (Book 2, Hadith 496), the Prophet Muhammad is reported to have said, "Do not waste water, even if you perform your ablution on the banks of an abundantly-flowing river." This Hadith underscores the importance of conserving water, a vital resource, regardless of its apparent abundance.

Sustainable Agriculture and Animal Welfare

The Quran emphasizes sustainable agricultural practices and the ethical treatment of animals, recognizing their intrinsic value and role within the ecological system. Sustainable agriculture is seen as a means to ensure food security and environmental health, while ethical treatment of animals reflects the compassion and mercy that Islam advocates.

Surah 6:141 advises, "And He it is who produces gardens trellised and untrellised, and date-palms, and crops of different shape and taste (its fruits and its seeds) and olives, and pomegranates, similar (in kind) and different (in taste). Eat of their fruit when they ripen, but pay the due thereof (its Zakat) on the day of its harvest, and waste not by extravagance. Verily, He likes not Al-Musrifun (those who waste by extravagance)." This verse encourages mindful harvesting and the payment of Zakat, linking agricultural practices with social and environmental responsibility.

The Hadith also addresses animal welfare. In Sahih Bukhari (Book 40, Hadith 551), the Prophet Muhammad is reported to have said, "Whoever is kind to the creatures of God is kind to himself." This Hadith reflects the broader ethical mandate to treat animals with kindness and respect.

Pollution and Environmental Degradation

The Quran condemns actions that lead to environmental degradation and pollution, advocating for cleanliness and the protection of natural habitats. Environmental degradation is viewed as a form of corruption (Fasad) that disrupts the balance and harmony of creation.

Surah 30:41 warns, "Corruption has appeared throughout the land and sea by [reason of] what the hands of people have earned so He may let them taste part of [the consequence of] what they have done that perhaps they will return [to righteousness]." This verse highlights the consequences of environmental corruption and serves as a call to restore and protect the natural world.

The Hadith literature also speaks against pollution. In Sunan Abi Dawood (Book 1, Hadith 68), the Prophet Muhammad is reported to have said, "Beware of the three acts that cause others to curse: relieving oneself in shaded places (that people utilize), in a walkway, or in a watering place." This Hadith underscores the importance of maintaining cleanliness and preventing pollution in communal spaces.

The Role of Human Innovation and Technology

The Quran encourages the use of human innovation and technology to enhance environmental stewardship, provided these advancements align with ethical principles and sustainability goals. Human creativity and intellect are viewed as gifts from Allah, to be used responsibly for the betterment of creation.

Surah 16:80-81 illustrates this perspective: "And Allah has made for you from your homes a place of rest and made for you from the hides of the animals tents which you find light on the day of travel and when you stop [for rest], and of their wool, fur, and hair [He has given you] furnishings and goods for use for a time. And Allah has made for you from that which He has created shadows and has made for you from the mountains, shelters, and has made for you garments which protect you from the heat and garments which protect you from your [enemy in] battle. Thus does He complete His favor upon you that you might submit [to Him]." These verses highlight the permissible use of natural resources and human ingenuity in creating beneficial technologies, emphasizing responsible use and ethical considerations.

Conclusion

The Quranic vision of environmental stewardship is comprehensive and deeply ethical, emphasizing the principles of balance, conservation, and compassionate use of resources. It calls upon humanity to act as responsible stewards of the Earth, maintaining the delicate equilibrium established by Allah. The Hadith literature further enriches this vision, offering practical guidance and reinforcing the ethical mandates of the Quran.

By embracing the Quranic teachings on environmental stewardship, individuals and communities are encouraged to adopt sustainable practices, protect natural habitats, and promote a harmonious relationship with the natural world. This holistic approach not only fulfills a divine mandate but also contributes to the well-being and sustainability of the planet.

References:

1. Surah 6:165 - Humanity's role as stewards of the Earth.
2. Surah 55:7-9 - Principle of balance in nature.
3. Sahih Bukhari, Book 72, Hadith 843 - Responsibility of stewardship.
4. Surah 7:31 - Encouragement of moderation and conservation.
5. Sahih Muslim, Book 2, Hadith 496 - Conservation of water.
6. Surah 6:141 - Sustainable agricultural practices and Zakat.
7. Sahih Bukhari, Book 40, Hadith 551 - Kindness to animals.
8. Surah 30:41 - Consequences of environmental corruption.
9. Sunan Abi Dawood, Book 1, Hadith 68 - Prohibition of polluting public spaces.
10. Surah 16:80-81 - Ethical use of human innovation and technology.

CHAPTER 14

The Quranic Approach to Health and Wellness

The Holistic Concept of Health in the Quran

The Quran presents a holistic approach to health and wellness, emphasizing the interconnectedness of physical, mental, and spiritual well-being. This comprehensive perspective is rooted in the belief that maintaining balance and harmony in all aspects of life is essential for overall health. The Quranic teachings advocate for preventive measures, healthy lifestyle choices, and the treatment of ailments, all within the framework of faith and ethical conduct.

Surah 2:195 advises, "And spend in the way of Allah and do not throw [yourselves] with your [own] hands into destruction [by refraining]. And do good; indeed, Allah loves the doers of good." This verse underscores the importance of proactive measures in maintaining health and well-being, highlighting the duty to preserve one's body and life.

Dietary Regulations and Nutrition

The Quran provides specific guidance on dietary regulations, promoting the consumption of wholesome and lawful (Halal) foods while prohibiting harmful and impure (Haram) substances. These dietary laws are designed to ensure physical health and spiritual purity, reflecting the broader principle of moderation and balance in consumption.

Surah 5:3 outlines the prohibitions on certain foods: "Prohibited to you are dead animals, blood, the flesh of swine, and that which has been dedicated to other than Allah, and [those animals] killed by strangling or by a violent blow or by a head-long fall or by the goring of horns, and those from which a wild animal has eaten, except what you [are able to] slaughter [before its death]." This verse establishes the dietary boundaries within which Muslims are to operate, emphasizing the importance of consuming Halal and wholesome food.

The Hadith literature further elaborates on dietary practices. In Sahih Bukhari (Book 76, Hadith 464), the Prophet Muhammad is reported to have said, "The son of Adam does not fill any vessel worse than his stomach. It is sufficient for the son of Adam to eat a few mouthfuls to keep him going. If he must fill it, then one-third for food, one-third for drink, and one-third for air." This Hadith highlights the principle of moderation in eating, which is crucial for maintaining physical health and well-being.

Hygiene and Cleanliness

Hygiene and cleanliness are paramount in Islamic teachings, encompassing both physical and spiritual dimensions. The Quran and Hadith emphasize regular practices of purification, which are integral to personal health and communal harmony.

Surah 2:222 states, "Indeed, Allah loves those who are constantly repentant and loves those who purify themselves." This verse links physical cleanliness with spiritual purity, underscoring the significance of hygiene in Islamic practice.

The Hadith literature provides detailed instructions on hygiene. In Sahih Muslim (Book 2, Hadith 432), the Prophet Muhammad is reported to have said, "Cleanliness is half of faith." This Hadith highlights the intrinsic value placed on cleanliness within Islam, reflecting its importance for both health and spirituality.

Mental Health and Emotional Well-being

The Quran addresses mental health and emotional well-being, recognizing the impact of stress, anxiety, and emotional distress on overall health. It offers guidance on fostering mental resilience and emotional balance through faith, prayer, and trust in Allah's wisdom.

Surah 94:5-6 offers reassurance: "For indeed, with hardship [will be] ease. Indeed, with hardship [will be] ease." These verses emphasize the transient nature of difficulties and the promise of relief, providing comfort and hope to those experiencing emotional distress.

The Hadith literature also addresses mental health. In Sahih Bukhari (Book 70, Hadith 545), the Prophet Muhammad is reported to have said, "There is no disease that Allah has created, except that He also has created its treatment." This Hadith underscores the importance of seeking remedies for mental and emotional ailments, reflecting the holistic approach to health in Islam.

Physical Exercise and Bodily Care

Physical exercise and bodily care are encouraged in Islam as means of maintaining health and vitality. The Quran advocates for the preservation of physical strength and the avoidance of harmful habits that can lead to physical deterioration.

Surah 4:29 advises, "And do not kill yourselves [or one another]. Indeed, Allah is to you ever Merciful." This verse underscores the duty to protect one's life and body, implicitly encouraging the adoption of healthy practices and the avoidance of harmful behaviors.

The Hadith literature provides practical examples of physical activity. In Sahih Bukhari (Book 52, Hadith 43), it is reported that the Prophet Muhammad encouraged swimming, archery, and horse riding, highlighting the importance of physical fitness and skill development.

The Role of Faith and Spiritual Practices in Health

Faith and spiritual practices play a crucial role in the Quranic approach to health and wellness. The Quran and Hadith emphasize the healing power of prayer, supplication (Dua), and reliance on Allah's mercy and wisdom.

Surah 41:44 states, "Say, 'It is, for those who believe, a guidance and cure.'" This verse highlights the dual role of the Quran as a source of spiritual guidance and healing, reflecting the integrative approach to health in Islam.

The Hadith literature also underscores the importance of spiritual practices in health. In Sahih Muslim (Book 26, Hadith 5461), the Prophet Muhammad is reported to have said, "Make use of medical treatment, for Allah has not made a disease without appointing a remedy for it, with the exception of one disease, namely old age." This Hadith encourages the use of both spiritual and medical remedies, advocating for a balanced approach to health care.

Conclusion

The Quranic approach to health and wellness is holistic and comprehensive, integrating physical, mental, and spiritual dimensions. It emphasizes preventive measures, moderation, cleanliness, and the importance of faith and spiritual practices in maintaining overall well-being. The Hadith literature enriches this perspective, offering practical guidance and reinforcing the ethical and spiritual principles outlined in the Quran.

By embracing the Quranic teachings on health and wellness, individuals are encouraged to adopt a balanced and integrative approach to health care, promoting harmony and well-being in all aspects of life. This holistic vision not only enhances personal health but also contributes to the collective well-being of the community.

References:

1. Surah 2:195 - Proactive measures in maintaining health.
2. Surah 5:3 - Dietary regulations and prohibitions.
3. Sahih Bukhari, Book 76, Hadith 464 - Principle of moderation in eating.
4. Surah 2:222 - Link between physical cleanliness and spiritual purity.
5. Sahih Muslim, Book 2, Hadith 432 - Cleanliness is half of faith.
6. Surah 94:5-6 - Reassurance during emotional distress.
7. Sahih Bukhari, Book 70, Hadith 545 - Seeking remedies for ailments.
8. Surah 4:29 - Duty to protect one's life and body.
9. Sahih Bukhari, Book 52, Hadith 43 - Encouragement of physical fitness.
10. Surah 41:44 - Quran as a source of guidance and healing.
11. Sahih Muslim, Book 26, Hadith 5461 - Use of medical and spiritual remedies.

CHAPTER 15

The Quranic Perspective on Interfaith Relations

The Principle of Religious Pluralism

The Quranic perspective on interfaith relations is anchored in the principle of religious pluralism, recognizing the existence and validity of diverse religious traditions. This perspective is rooted in the acknowledgment that human beings have been endowed with free will and the capacity to choose their own paths, including their religious beliefs. The Quran advocates for respectful dialogue and coexistence among different faith communities.

Surah 2:256 asserts, "There is no compulsion in religion. The right course has become clear from the wrong." This verse underscores the Quranic principle that faith cannot be compelled, and that genuine belief must be a product of personal conviction and choice.

Recognition of the People of the Book

The Quran specifically acknowledges the People of the Book (Ahl al-Kitab), referring to Jews and Christians, and accords them a special status. This recognition is based on the shared Abrahamic heritage and the commonalities in the core teachings of monotheism, morality, and justice.

Surah 3:64 invites the People of the Book to a common understanding: "Say, 'O People of the Scripture, come to a word that is equitable between us and you – that we will not worship except Allah and not associate anything with Him and not take one another as lords instead of Allah.'" This verse emphasizes the call for mutual respect and cooperation based on shared values and monotheistic belief.

The Hadith literature further supports this inclusive approach. In Sahih Bukhari (Book 60, Hadith 25), the Prophet Muhammad is reported to have said, "Whoever believes in Allah and the Last Day and does righteous deeds, will have their reward with their Lord, and there will be no fear for them, nor will they grieve." This Hadith underscores the Quranic view that righteousness and faith are not confined to a single religious community.

Respectful Dialogue and Coexistence

The Quran advocates for respectful dialogue and peaceful coexistence with people of different faiths. It encourages Muslims to engage in constructive conversations, seeking common ground and understanding while maintaining their own beliefs and practices.

Surah 16:125 advises, "Invite to the way of your Lord with wisdom and good instruction, and argue with them in a way that is best. Indeed, your Lord is most knowing of who has strayed from His way, and He is most knowing of who is [rightly] guided." This verse highlights the importance of wisdom, kindness, and respect in interfaith dialogue.

The Hadith literature reinforces this approach. In Sunan Abi Dawood (Book 41, Hadith 4885), it is narrated that the Prophet Muhammad said, "I have been sent with a religion of ease." This Hadith reflects the Prophet's emphasis on ease and flexibility in religious practice, promoting a spirit of tolerance and understanding in interfaith interactions.

Common Ethical and Moral Foundations

The Quran recognizes the common ethical and moral foundations shared by various religious traditions. It emphasizes universal values such as justice, compassion, honesty, and charity, which form the basis for mutual respect and cooperation among different faith communities.

Surah 5:8 enjoins, "O you who have believed, be persistently standing firm for Allah, witnesses in justice, and do not let the hatred of a people prevent you from being just. Be just; that is nearer to righteousness. And fear Allah; indeed, Allah is Acquainted with what you do." This verse underscores the imperative of justice and fairness, even towards those with whom one may have differences.

The Hadith literature also emphasizes shared ethical values. In Sahih Muslim (Book 32, Hadith 6251), the Prophet Muhammad is reported to have said, "He who does not show mercy to others will not be shown mercy." This Hadith highlights the universal value of compassion, which transcends religious boundaries and fosters mutual respect and understanding.

The Concept of Universal Brotherhood

The Quran promotes the concept of universal brotherhood, emphasizing the unity of humanity and the importance of peaceful coexistence. This principle is rooted in the belief that all human beings are created by Allah and are part of a single human family.

Surah 49:13 declares, "O mankind, indeed We have created you from male and female and made you peoples and tribes that you may know one another. Indeed, the most noble of you in the sight of Allah is the most righteous of you. Indeed, Allah is Knowing and Acquainted." This verse highlights the diversity of humanity as a means for mutual recognition and learning, rather than division and conflict.

The Hadith literature echoes this sentiment. In Sahih Bukhari (Book 8, Hadith 73), the Prophet Muhammad is reported to have said, "The best among you are those who have the best manners and character." This Hadith underscores the importance of character and conduct, promoting a spirit of mutual respect and cooperation among all people.

The Prohibition of Religious Hostility

The Quran explicitly prohibits religious hostility and encourages Muslims to maintain peaceful and respectful relations with people of other faiths. It condemns acts of aggression and enmity based on religious differences, advocating instead for patience, forgiveness, and reconciliation.

Surah 60:8 states, "Allah does not forbid you from those who do not fight you because of religion and do not expel you from your homes – from being righteous toward them and acting justly toward them. Indeed, Allah loves those who act justly." This verse emphasizes the importance of just and fair treatment of others, regardless of their religious beliefs.

The Hadith literature provides further guidance on avoiding religious hostility. In Sahih Muslim (Book 32, Hadith 6250), the Prophet Muhammad is reported to have said, "Do not wish for an encounter with the enemy; pray to Allah to grant you security." This Hadith reflects the Prophet's emphasis on seeking peace and avoiding conflict.

Conclusion

The Quranic perspective on interfaith relations is grounded in the principles of respect, justice, and peaceful coexistence. It recognizes the diversity of religious traditions and promotes dialogue, understanding, and mutual respect. The Hadith literature enriches this perspective, providing practical guidance and reinforcing the ethical and moral principles outlined in the Quran.

By embracing the Quranic teachings on interfaith relations, individuals and communities are encouraged to foster a spirit of tolerance and cooperation, building bridges of understanding and harmony among diverse faith communities. This approach not only enhances social cohesion but also reflects the Quranic vision of a just and compassionate world.

References:

1. Surah 2:256 - No compulsion in religion.
2. Surah 3:64 - Invitation to common understanding with the People of the Book.
3. Sahih Bukhari, Book 60, Hadith 25 - Reward for those who believe and do righteous deeds.
4. Surah 16:125 - Invitation with wisdom and good instruction.
5. Sunan Abi Dawood, Book 41, Hadith 4885 - Religion of ease.
6. Surah 5:8 - Standing firm in justice.
7. Sahih Muslim, Book 32, Hadith 6251 - Mercy towards others.
8. Surah 49:13 - Unity of humanity and mutual recognition.
9. Sahih Bukhari, Book 8, Hadith 73 - Importance of manners and character.
10. Surah 60:8 - Prohibition of religious hostility.
11. Sahih Muslim, Book 32, Hadith 6250 - Avoiding conflict and seeking peace.

APPENDIX

Appendix: Supplementary Analysis of Quranic Exegesis and Hadith Literature

The Structure and Methodology of Quranic Exegesis

Quranic exegesis (Tafsir) is an intricate and profound discipline aimed at elucidating the meanings, contexts, and implications of the Quranic text. The methodology employed in Tafsir integrates various interpretative tools, including linguistic analysis, historical context, and cross-references within the Quran and Hadith.

One foundational principle in Tafsir is the interpretation of the Quran by the Quran itself, wherein ambiguous verses are clarified by other verses. This method is reinforced by Surah 3:7: "It is He who has sent down to you, [O Muhammad], the Book; in it are verses [that are] precise - they are the foundation of the Book - and others unspecific. As for those in whose hearts is deviation [from truth], they will follow that of it which is unspecific, seeking discord and seeking an interpretation [suitable to them]. And no one knows its [true] interpretation except Allah. But those firm in knowledge say, 'We believe in it. All [of it] is from our Lord.' And no one will be reminded except those of understanding."

Linguistic and Rhetorical Analysis

The linguistic and rhetorical analysis of the Quran is pivotal in Tafsir, given the Quran's unparalleled eloquence and stylistic uniqueness. Exegetes meticulously analyze the language, syntax, and literary devices used in the Quran to uncover deeper meanings and subtleties. This approach is illustrated in the study of the Quranic use of Saj' (rhymed prose), which enhances the text's aesthetic and mnemonic qualities.

Surah 54:17 highlights the Quran's accessibility and ease of memorization: "And We have certainly made the Quran easy for remembrance, so is there any who will remember?" This verse underscores the importance of the Quran's linguistic features in facilitating its comprehension and retention.

Historical Context and Asbab al-Nuzul

Understanding the historical context and the circumstances of revelation (Asbab al-Nuzul) is essential for accurate exegesis. The Asbab al-Nuzul provide insights into the specific events and situations that prompted the revelation of particular verses, thereby clarifying their intended meanings and applications.

For example, Surah 2:217 was revealed in response to the questions about the permissibility of fighting during the sacred months: "They ask you about the sacred month - about fighting therein. Say, 'Fighting therein is great [sin], but averting [people] from the way of Allah and disbelief in Him and [preventing access to] al-Masjid al-Haram and the expulsion of its people therefrom are greater [evil] in the sight of Allah. And fitnah is greater than killing.' And they will continue to fight you until they turn you back from your religion if they are able."

The Role of Hadith in Tafsir

The Hadith literature is indispensable in Quranic exegesis, providing context, elaboration, and exemplification of the Quranic verses. The sayings and actions of the Prophet Muhammad, recorded in Hadith collections, serve as a practical guide for interpreting and applying the Quranic teachings.

In Sahih Bukhari (Book 65, Hadith 1), the Prophet Muhammad explains the significance of seeking knowledge: "The seeking of knowledge is obligatory for every Muslim." This Hadith underscores the importance of understanding the Quran and Hadith as a combined source of Islamic knowledge and guidance.

Comparative Exegesis

Comparative exegesis involves examining the interpretations of various classical and contemporary scholars to gain a comprehensive understanding of the Quranic text. This approach highlights the diversity of thought within Islamic scholarship and allows for a more nuanced interpretation of the Quran.

Classical exegetes such as Ibn Kathir, Al-Tabari, and Al-Qurtubi have made significant contributions to the field of Tafsir, each offering unique perspectives based on their methodologies and contexts. Contemporary scholars continue to build on this rich tradition, addressing modern challenges and questions.

Conclusion

The study of Quranic exegesis and Hadith literature is a dynamic and multifaceted endeavor that requires a deep understanding of linguistic, historical, and contextual factors. By employing rigorous methodologies and drawing on a wide range of scholarly interpretations, Muslims can gain a profound and nuanced understanding of their sacred texts. This appendix has provided a brief overview of the principles and practices of Tafsir, highlighting its critical role in the interpretation and application of the Quran and Hadith.

Appendix

In this appendix I have chosen 20 thematic verses from Zayds poetry and compared them with the verses of the Quran. You will notice how uncannily they resemble the likeness of Zayds composition. Due to the repetitive nature of the Quranic verses many verses are quite similar to the chosen theme of Zayds composition. This is why I also included a few other verses which are in close resemblance with Zayds poetry. To keep the length of this appendix short I have quoted the full verses only in cases where the similarities are unusually close. For the other verses, I only included the main messages. You may consult the English translation of the Holy Quran to read the complete verses. Needless to say, I only cited a handful of verses. You may spend some time searching the Holy Quran for other verses which are closely alike to the verses of Zayds poetry

[*Please note*: Unless mentioned otherwise, the quoted verses from the Quran are from Abdullah Yusuf Alis translation of the Holy Quran. Note also that the original translation of Yusuf Ali refers Allah as God. The internet version of this translation refers only Allah. My essay is based on the original version of Yusuf Alis translation. You may click here to verify the verses quoted:

http://www.usc.edu/dept/MSA/quran/]

For Readers convenience excerpts from Zayds poetry are quoted here again (Part 3/5):

Ibn Ishaq (pp.100-101)

Zayd b. Amr. B. Nufayl composed the following poem about leaving his people and the torment he received from them:

> Am I to worship one lord or a thousand?
> If there are as many as you claim,
> I renounce al-Lat and al-Uzza both of them
> As any strong-minded person would.
> I will not worship al-Uzza and her two daughters,
> Nor will I visit the two images of the Banu Amr.

I will not worship Hubal though he was our lord
In the days when I had little sense.
I wondered (for in the night much is strange
Which in daylight is plain to the discerning),
That God had annihilated many men
Whose deeds were thoroughly evil
And spared others through the piety of a people
So that a little child could grow in manhood.
A man may languish for a time and then recover
As the branch of a tree revives after the rain.
I serve my Lord the compassionate
That the forgiving Lord may pardon my sin,
So, keep to the fear of God your Lord;
While you hold to that you will not perish.
You will see the pious living in gardens,
While for the infidels, hell fire is burning.
Shamed in life, when they die
Their breasts will contract in anguish.

Zayd also said: (143)
To God I give my praise and thanksgiving,
A sure word that will not fail as long as time lasts,
To the heavenly King there is no God beyond Him
And no lord can draw near to Him.
Beware, O men, of what follows death!
You can hide nothing from God.
Beware of putting another beside God,
For the upright way has become clear.
Merry I implore, others trust in jinn,
But thou, my God, art our Lord and our hope.
I am satisfied with thee, O God, as a Lord,

And will not worship another God beside thee.

Thou of thy goodness and mercy

Didst send a messenger to Moses as a herald.

Thou saidst to him, Go thou and Aaron,

And summon Pharaoh the tyrant to run to God

And say to him, did you spread out this (earth) without support,

Until it stood fast as it does?

Say to him Did you raise this (heaven) without support?

What a fine builder then you were!

Say to him Did you set the moon in the middle thereof

As a light to guide when night covered it?

Say to him, who sent forth the sun by day

So that the earth it touched reflected its splendor?

Say to him, who planted seeds in the dust

That herbage might grow and wax great?

And brought forth its seeds in the head of the plant?

Therein are signs for the understanding.

Thou in thy kindness did deliver Jonah

Who spent nights in the belly of the fish.

Though I glorify thy name, I often repeat

O Lord of creatures, bestow thy gifts and mercy upon me

And bless my sons and property.

[(143) Ibn Hishams note (ibn Ishaq p.713): These verses really belong to an ode of Umayya b. Abul-Salt, except for the first two, the fifth, and the last verse. The second half of the first verse does not come via I.I.]

Here is another sample verse of Zayd b. Amr (ibn Ishaq, p.102):

And Zayd said:

I submit myself to him to whom

The earth which bears mighty rocks is subject.
He spread it out and when He saw it was settled
Upon the waters, He fixed the mountains on it.
I submit myself to Him to whom clouds which bear
Sweet water are subject
When they are borne along to a land
They obediently pour copious rain upon it.

Here are the comparisons of Zayds verses with the verses of the Holy Quran:

1. Zayd wrote: Am I to worship one lord or a thousand?
The Holy Quran says:
Muslims God is one God (that is Allah only); those who do not believe in the hereafter are proud16:22
016.022 Your Allah is one Allah: as to those who believe not in the Hereafter, their hearts refuse to know, and they are arrogant.
Other similar verses in the Holy Quran:
Cannot set up religious leaders and scholars as Lords; God had commanded to worship only one God 9:31
None can change the words of God 10:64
Quran teaches to worship none but God and Muhammad is a Warner who brought glad tidings 11:2
Do not worship two gods; there is only one God, worship Him alone...16:51
All messengers were inspired to worship one God only 21:25
There is only one God and all should bow to Islam...21:108
There is only one God 37:4
Muhammad is a warner; there is no God but one supreme38:65
Muhammad's religion is devoted to God alone 39:14
Muhammad is commanded to worship God only3 9:11

Can't have many conflicting partners; one should serve only one master (this verse is used by the Quran only followers e.g., Rashad Khalifa) 39:29

God is one and the only...112:1

2. Zayd wrote: Not worshipping al-Lat, al-Uzza and her two daughters

The Holy Quran says:

All prophets were, at times inspired by Satan (this is the abrogating verse for 53:19-20 dealing with Al-Lat, al-Uzza and Manat were goddesses (this verse is believed to be inspired by Satan and so abrogated by 22:52) ...53:19-23

053.019 Have ye seen Lat. and 'Uzza,

053.020 And another, the third (goddess), Manat?

053.021 What! for you the male sex, and for Him, the female?

053.022 Behold, such would be indeed a division most unfair!

053.023 These are nothing but names which ye have devised, - ye and your fathers, - for which Allah has sent down no authority (whatever). They follow nothing but conjecture and what their own souls desire! - Even though there has already come to them Guidance from their Lord!

Other similar verses from the Holy Quran:

All prophets were, at times inspired by Satan (this is the abrogating verse for 53:19-20 dealing with goddesses al-Lat, Uzza, Manat) ...22:52

False daughters were assigned to God...52:39

God is not of female sex...53:21

3. Zayd wrote: God annihilated many men whose deeds were thoroughly evil

The Holy Quran says:

God had annihilated many generations before Muhammad's generation 6:6

006.006 See they not how many of those before them We did destroy? - generations We had established on the earth, in strength such as We have not given to you - for whom We poured out rain from the skies in abundance, and gave (fertile) streams flowing beneath their (feet): yet for their sins We destroyed them, and raised in their wake fresh generations (to succeed them).

Other similar verses from the Holy Quran:

God annihilated many communities while they were awake or asleep 7:4

God annihilated many generations and made the current generation to inherit earth just to test them 10:13-14

God has annihilated many generations before whom no one can trace 19:98

God has destroyed many previous generations 20:128

In the past, God had punished many a population...22:48

God destroyed all the community of the unbelievers, yet they disbelieve 21:6

God utterly destroyed many populations before...21:11

God completely wiped out the runaway transgressors 21:15

In the past, God destroyed many populations, made wells idle, and neglected and destroyed lofty and well-built castles...22:45

God had destroyed many generations before 32:26

God destroyed many generations before; their call for help was in vain 38:3

God annihilated those powerful people 43:8

In the past God seized and punished people for disobeying their messengers 40:22

God had annihilated many communities before Muhammad was sent 46:27

In the past, God had annihilated many a powerful generation 50:36

God had annihilated the earlier generations 77:16

The past disbelievers of God received a severe retribution from God 64:5

In the past God had severely punished the past unbelievers 67:18

4. Zayd wrote: And spared the others

The Holy Quran says:

God may punish or redeem the others 9:106

009.106 There are (yet) others, held in suspense for the command of Allah, whether He will punish them, or turn in mercy to them: and Allah is All-Knowing, Wise.

Other similar verse from the Holy Quran: God has a predetermined plan for the unbelievers, that's why He does not annihilate them immediately 20:130

5. Zayd wrote: the branch of a tree revives after the rain

The Holy Quran says:

God sends down rain from sky for plants to grow and gives life to the dead land (part of water cycle?) ...50:9-11

050.009 And We send down from the sky rain charted with blessing, and We produce therewith gardens and Grain for harvests;

050.010 And tall (and stately) palm-trees, with shoots of fruit-stalks, piled one over another; -

050.011 As sustenance for (Allah's) Servants; - and We give (new) life therewith to land that is dead: Thus will be the Resurrection.

Other similar verses from the Holy Quran:

In the creation of the heavens and the earth, in the alternation of the night and the day, in the sailing of the ships through the ocean, the rain from the sky, and the springing of vegetation on a dead earth, the

scattered beasts, the change of winds and clouds are the signs of
God...2:164

God produces rain from the sky to grow agricultural products 6:99

God sends the winds to carry the heavily laden clouds to fall as rain in a
dead land to produce agriculture (part of water cycle?)...7:57

God sends the fertile wind to cause the rain that makes the vegetation
to grow (part of water cycle?)...15:22

The rain, the plants on earth and the hay are the signs of God; he is all-
powerful 18:45

God sends down rains and is cognizant 22:63

God sent down rain from the sky; rain soaked in soil, then drains off
23:18

God drives rain to perched soils to feed the cattle...32:27

God sends down rain from the sky and causes the spring to flow and
causes the vegetation to grow (part of water cycle?)...39:21

With rain God gives life to a barren earth, He can also give life to the
dead...43:11

God revives a land after it had died 57:17

6. Zayd wrote: So, keep to the fear of God, hold to that you will not perish

The Holy Quran says:

Fear God and God alone...2:41

002.041 And believe in what I reveal, confirming the revelation which
is with you, and be not the first to reject Faith therein, nor sell My Signs
for a small price; and fear Me, and Me alone.

Other similar verses from the Holy Quran:

Can't die except as a Muslim; fear Allah as He should be feared ...3:102

Those who fear God dwell in heaven permanently...3:198

Fear God and don not create trouble in an ordered world7:56

God sent earthquake to almost topple the mountains as a warning to fear God...7:171

The true believers heart tremble with fear at the mention of God and their faith is strengthened whenever they hear the recitation of the Quran8:2

Believers should fear God and follow the truthful believers 9:119

Fear God for the terrible judgment day...22:1

A true believer's heart trembles in fear when he hears the name of God22:35

Repent and fear God30:31

Those who have knowledge truly fear God35:28

God's earth is spacious; fear God; He is on the side of the good doers39:10

Fear God as much you are able to do so...64:16

There is a great reward for those who fear the unseen God...67:12

Quran is a message for the God-fearing people 69:47

If you fear and obey God, then He will forgive you...71:3-4

He who gives charity and fears God is the best...92:5-6

7. Zayd wrote: pious living in gardens. For the infidels, hell fire is burning

The Holy Quran says:

Garden will be brought to righteous and hell fire for the evil doers 26:90-95

026.090 "To the righteous, the Garden will be brought near,
026.091 "And to those straying in Evil, the Fire will be placed in full view;

026.092 "And it shall be said to them: 'Where are the (gods) ye worshipped-
026.093 "'Besides Allah? Can they help you or help themselves?'
026.094 "Then they will be thrown headlong into the (Fire),- they and those straying in Evil,

026.095 "And the whole hosts of Iblis together.

Other similar verses from the Holy Quran:

Their reward is the gardens of eternity, they will dwell therein forever; God is pleased with them and they are pleased with God and there is a great reward for fearing God...98:8

For the righteous there are gardens in nearness to God...3:15

Gardens with rivers flowing underneath for the believers...3:136

The believers will profit by following Islam; they will be rewarded with gardens with river flowing underneath, eternal home for the believers...5:119

God promises paradise (beautiful mansions in the garden of Eden) to the believing men and women 9:72

Believers will enter the gardens of Eden together with their righteous parents, spouses and children; angels will accompany the believers who enter there...13:23
For the believers...gardens beneath which flows river...13:35

Believers will be admitted to the gardens beneath which river flows; they will be adorned with bracelets of gold and pearls and their garments will be of silk...22.23

God will be the supreme judge on the resurrection day; garden of delight is for the believers 22:56

Fire will be placed in full view 26:91

Garden will be brought to righteous 26:90

Gardens as hospitable homes are for the believers...32:19

Unbelievers will be in the abode of fire; they will be forced back there if they try to escape...32:20

The believers will be in gardens of eternity; they will be adorned with bracelets of gold and pearls and their garments will be of silk 35:33

There is un-ending fire of hell for rejecting God; they will not die; penalty for them will not be lightened 35:36

For the believers there will be garden of joy, cool shades of wood, reclining on thrones, all fruits are for enjoyment, peace from God 36:55-58

Sinners will be set apart; they will embrace fire 36:60-64

For the sincere and devoted servants of God there will be sustenance (in Paradise), fruits, honor, dignity, garden of felicity, they will face each other on thrones, pass around a cup from a clear flowing fountain, crystal white delicious drink, no headache, no intoxication, chaste women 36:41-50

Believers will see the unbelievers being roasted in fire 37:51-55

God sent an Arabic Quran to warn. Some home will be in garden and some will be in blazing fire...42:7

The believers and their wives enter garden, pass round dishes and goblets of gold, everything all the souls could desire, all that eyes could delight in...43:70-72

The sinners will be punished; they will remain in hell forever...43:74

Believers will be admitted to the Gardens; the unbelievers will enjoy this world like cattle eats and they will have their abode in fire...47:12

For the believers there will be gardens to dwell in, beneath which rivers flow; their sins remitted...48:5

The righteous will be in the garden of happiness ...52:17

The righteous will be in the midst of gardens and rivers and in the presence of an omnipotent sovereign...54:55

Believers will recline on carpets with inner linings of rich brocade; the fruits of the garden will be nearby...55:54

In return for fighting for God, He forgives sins and promises beautiful mansions in the gardens of eternity...61:12

For the believers, God will remove ills (sins) from them; give them gardens to dwell in there forever under which rivers flow...64:9

The disbelievers will live in hell fire for ever...64:10

There are the gardens of delight in the presence of God...68:34

God has fetters to bind the unbelievers and then burn them in fire and feed them with food that is hard to swallow...73:12

For the disbelievers, God has prepared shackles, chains and a blazing hellfire 76:4

For the believers there will be gardens...85:11

They will be on a high garden...88:10

8. Zayd wrote: ..breasts will contract in anguish

The Holy Quran says:
God opens the breasts of those who accept Islam; those who strays gets their breasts contracted, as if climbing in the air and gasping for breath...6:125

006.125 Those whom Allah (in His plan) willeth to guide, - He openeth their breast to Islam; those whom He willeth to leave straying, - He maketh their breast close and constricted, as if they had to climb up to the skies: thus doth Allah (heap) the penalty on those who refuse to believe.

Other similar verses from the Holy Quran:

God will confuse the hearts and eyes of the disbelievers6:110

Through the narration of the previous disbelievers of their prophets, God shows the example that He seals the heart of the disbelievers 7:101

God seals the hearts of the transgressors...10:74

No soul can believe except by the will of God; He will place doubt and obscurity in the heart of unbelievers...10:100

God seals up hearts of those who do not understand...30:59

Hearts will be in agitation...79:8

The unbeliever's heart is shielded by his by sins 83:14

9. Zayd wrote: there is no God beyond Him

The Holy Quran says:

There is only one God and all should bow to Islam...21:108

021.108 Say: "What has come to me by inspiration is that your Allah is One Allah: will ye therefore bow to His Will (in Islam)?"

There is no God but He, the supreme 27:26

027.026 "Allah! - there is no god but He!- Lord of the Throne Supreme!"

Other similar verses from the Holy Quran:

Every life returns to God, the ultimate judge 6:62

There is no similitude for God 16:74

Can't set up any God besides Allah 17:22

If there were gods besides God, there would be chaos 21:22

All messengers were inspired to worship one God only 21:25

Sovereignty belongs to God; there is no God but Him. Everything will perish except God's face 28:88

No helper or protector besides God29:22

There is no God but He 35:3

There is only one God 37:4

Muhammad is a warner; there is no God but one supreme 38:65

God is the most high, the most great...42:4

God is the only deity in the heavens and the only deity on earth...43:84

God is the Lord of the heavens and the earth and everything between them 44:7

God is the first and the last (alpha and omega)...57:3

All Kingships is with God 67:1

God is one and the only...112:1

None is like God...112:4

10. Zayd wrote: You can hide nothing from God

The Holy Quran says:

God has a clear record of everything; nothing is hidden from him 27:75

027.075 **YUSUFALI:** Nor is there aught of the unseen, in heaven or earth, but is (recorded) in a clear record.

PICKTHAL: And there is nothing hidden in the heaven or the earth but it is in a clear Record.

SHAKIR: And there is nothing concealed in the heaven and the earth but it is in a clear book.

Other similar verses from the Holy Quran:

God knows what you hide or reveal...3:29

The hypocrites pretend to be believers when they meet Muhammad but they are actually against the faith; God knows all that they hide...5:61

Can't hide from God: He knows the innermost secrets of our hearts...11:5

God knows what is secret and what is hidden...20:7

God knows what is in your open speech and what you hide in your heart...21:110

God knows all hidden and open secrets; He has no partner 23:92

God knows everything that you hide and reveal 27:74

God is the knower of all things hidden and open...32:6

God knows what the unbelievers hide and what they disclose 36:75

God knows all things secret and open...59:22

God knows the innermost secret of everyone 64:4

Whether declared or secret, God is aware of our innermost thoughts 67:13

11. Zayd wrote: the upright way has become clear

The Holy Quran says:

No compulsion in religion; the truth is clear from error...2:256

002.256 Let there be no compulsion in religion: Truth stands out clear from Error: whoever rejects evil and believes in Allah hath grasped the most trustworthy hand-hold, that never breaks. And Allah heareth and knoweth all things.

Other similar verses from the Holy Quran:

Quran is a clear revelation; the disbelievers are evil people...2:99

The Quran is a clear book...5:15

The Quran makes things clear...15:1

Quran is a clear sign from God...22:16

God has made things clear in the Quran and He guides to a straight path whomever He wills 24:46

The Quran makes things clear 26:1

Muhammad does not recite any poetry; the Quran is a clear message 36:69

God has sent down clear revelations (Quran)57:9

The straight and the right religion involves the worshipping of God sincerely, be true to faith, establish regular prayers and practice regular charity (Zakat)...98:5

12. Zayd wrote: And will not worship another God beside thee

The Holy Quran says:
Can't worship anything other than God; Islam is the only right religion...12:40

012.040 "If not Him, ye worship nothing but names which ye have named,- ye and your fathers,- for which Allah hath sent down no authority: the command is for none but Allah: He hath commanded that ye worship none but Him: that is the right religion, but most men understand not..

Other similar verses from the Holy Quran:
Gods covenant with the Children of Israel (i.e., the Jews) were: 1. to worship God only 2. honor parents 3. regard relatives, orphans and the poor 3. treat people amicably 4. observe contact prayers 5. give obligatory charity 5. no shedding of blood 6. not to evict each other from homes...2:83-84
It is not possible for the people of the Book to worship any idol other than God alone 3:79
Worship God alone; you will ultimately go back to Him 7:29
Worship only God privately and publicly 7:55
Cannot set up religious leaders and scholars as lords; God had commanded to worship only one God 9:31
Muhammad does not worship that others worship; he worships only God 10:104
Quran teaches to worship none but God and Muhammad is a Warner who brought glad tidings 11:2

God sent apostle to every people; Muhammad had been commanded to worship God and nothing else; God guided some but made errors on some...16:36

Do not worship two gods; there is only one God, worship Him alone...16:51

All messengers were inspired to worship one God only 21:25

Muhammad is commanded to worship God only39:11

The believers must worship God even if the disbelievers dislike it 40:14

Muhammad is forbidden to worship any idol; commanded to worship God only 40:66

Muhammad is to worship only God; he has neither power to harm nor to guide people 72:20-21

The entire Sura Kafiirun (Sura 109)

13. Zayd wrote: a messenger to Moses as a herald

The Holy Quran writes:

They (Moses and his servant) met Gods angel there (at the junction of the two seas)18:65

018.065 So they found one of Our servants, on whom We had bestowed Mercy from Ourselves and whom We had taught knowledge from Our own Presence.

018.065 So they found one of Our servants, on whom We had bestowed Mercy from Ourselves and whom We had taught knowledge from Our own Presence.

Other similar verses from the Holy Quran:

God spoke to Moses and chose him as His messenger among his people 7:144

God spoke to Moses directly...4:164

God spoke directly with Moses and he was the first to believe in Islam...7:143

Moses sought the permission of the angel to follow him to learn from him 18:66

God sent Moses and his brother Aaron with His revelation and a profound proof 23:45

 God chose Moses as a messenger and told him to worship Him alone20:14

God sent Moses the Book and made Aaron, his brother his assistant (minister) 25:35

14. Zayd wrote: Say to Pharaoh: Did you spread out this earth without supports.?

The Holy Quran says:

God raised heavens without pillars (first?), (then?) established His throne, (then?) subjected the sun and (then?) the moon to run their courses; He regulates all affairs...13:2

013.002 Allah is He Who raised the heavens without any pillars that ye can see; is firmly established on the throne (of authority); He has subjected the sun and the moon (to his Law)! Each one runs (its course) for a term appointed. He doth regulate all affairs, explaining the signs in detail, that ye may believe with certainty in the meeting with your Lord.

 Other similar verses from the Holy Quran:

God created heavens without pillars (supports) so that you can see and He set mountains firm for the earth not to shake; He set scattered beasts of every kind in pairs...31:10

God agreed to appoint Aaron, Moses brother to be his assistant and assured Mosess victory against the Pharaoh28:35

God asked Moses to go to Pharaoh to redeem him79:17-19

15. Zayd wrote: .set the moon in the middle thereof As a light to guide when night covered it

The Holy Quran says:
God made the moon a light (i.e. moon gives light) in the midst of heavens and the sun a lamp...71:15-16

071.015 "'See ye not how Allah has created the seven heavens one above another,
071.016 "'And made the moon a light in their midst, and made the sun as a (Glorious) Lamp?

Other similar verses from the Holy Quran:
God made the constellations in the sky and put a lamp (the sun) and a shining moon (i.e., the moon gives light) 25:61
God made night and day, the sun and the moon are subject to man...16:12
God created the sun and the moon for day and night and for the reckoning of time 6:96
God made the sun a shining glory and the moon a beauty and having its stages; the sun and the moon are used to reckon the years and time 10:5
The sun and the moon are subject to courses...14:33
God merges night into day and subjected the sun and the moon running its courses...31:29
God has appointed mansions (or stages) for the moon till she returns like an old weathered palm leaf 36:39
The sun is not permitted to catch up with the moon; the night cannot outstrip the day 6:40

16. Zayd wrote: Who planted seeds in the dust that herbage might grow

The Holy Quran says:
God has created His signs in plant and vegetable 13:4
013.004 And in the earth are tracts (diverse though) neighboring, and gardens of vines and fields sown with corn, and palm trees - growing out of single roots or otherwise: watered with the same water, yet some of them We make more excellent than others to eat. Behold, verily in these things there are signs for those who understand!

It is not in the power of men to cause the growth of plants and trees 27:60

027.060 Or, Who has created the heavens and the earth, and Who sends you down rain from the sky? Yea, with it We cause to grow well-planted orchards full of beauty of delight: it is not in your power to cause the growth of the trees in them. (Can there be another) god besides Allah? Nay, they are a people who swerve from justice.

Other similar verses from the Holy Quran:
The rain, the plants on earth and the hay are the signs of God; he is all-powerful 18:45
God sends down rain from sky for plants to grow and gives life to the dead land (part of water cycle?)...50:9-11
God has germinated us like plants from earth...71:17

17. Zayd wrote: Therein are signs for the understanding

The Holy Quran says

The Quran is full of blessings and book of signs; only men of understanding can resolve the genuine doubts in Quran 38:29

038.029 (Here is) a Book which We have sent down unto thee, full of blessings, that they may mediate on its Signs, and that men of understanding may receive admonition.

Other similar verses from the Holy Quran:

In the creation of the heavens and the earth, in the alternation of the night and the day, in the sailing of the ships through the ocean, the rain from the sky, and the springing of vegetation on dead earth, the scattered beasts, the change of winds and clouds are the signs of God...2:164

The earth and the alternation of night and day, are the signs of God ...3:190

The alternation of night and day and all that on earth are the signs of God ...10:6

The rain, the plants on earth and the hay are the signs of God; He is all-powerful 18:45

Signs of God is in cattle of pastures; God created humans from earth, they will end in earth and will be brought out in earth again...20:54

On earth, there are signs of faith...51:20

18. Zayd wrote: ...deliver Jonah who spent nights in the belly of fish

The Holy Quran says:

God saved Jonah (Dhan Nun) from the darkness (belly of a big fish) 21:87-88

021.087 And remember Zun-nun, when he departed in wrath: He imagined that We had no power over him! But he cried through the deptHs of darkness, "There is no god but thou: glory to thee: I was indeed wrong!"

021.088 So We listened to him: and delivered him from distress: and thus do We deliver those who have faith.

Other similar verses from the Holy Quran:
Because of his rebellion, a big fish swallowed Jonah 37:142
But Jonah repented and prayed to God and God rescued him from the big fish 37:143-144
God made the fish throw Jonah into a desert 37:145

19. Zayd wrote: The earth spread out. Fixed mountains on it

The Holy Quran says:
God made earth spread out like a carpet (flat), set mountains firm...15:19

015.019 And the earth We have spread out (like a carpet); set thereon mountains firm and immovable; and produced therein all kinds of things in due balance.

Other similar verses from the holy Quran
God spread out the earth (flat), set mountains, put night as a veil...13:3
God set up mountains firm lest the earth shake...16:15
God made earth like a carpet spread out (flat); God created diverse pairs of plants...20:53
God set mountains high lest the earth shake with them and laid the highways to guide people...21:31
God made the earth to live in; He made the rivers on earth, set the immovable mountains and the separating waters 27:61

The earth is like a carpet spread out (flat) and God built roads and channels in it...43:10

God spread out earth (flat) and set mountains standing firm...50:7

God made mountains standing firm and provided sweet water...77:27

God put mountains as pegs (or stabilizers) to hold the earth in place...78:7

The earth is spread out (flat)...88:20

God established mountains firmly fixed...79:32

Mountains are fixed firmly...79:32

Mountains are set firm by the power of God...88:19

20. Zayd wrote:. clouds which bear sweet water?

The Holy Quran says:
God sends down water from the clouds to grow vegetables and gardens..78:14-16

078.014 And do We not send down from the clouds water in abundance,
078.015 That We may produce therewith corn and vegetables,
078.016 And gardens of luxurious growth?

Other similar verses from the Holy Quran:
God sends the winds to carry the heavily laden clouds to fall as rain in a dead land to produce agriculture (part of water cycle?)...7:57

God moves clouds and causes rain and snow24:43

God sends winds, winds raise the cloud; God spreads the clouds in sky, breaks clouds in fragments until rain drops (part of water cycle?)...30:48

God made mountains standing firm and provided sweet water...77:27

References:

1. Surah 3:7 - Interpretation of the Quran by the Quran itself.

2. Surah 54:17 - The Quran's accessibility and ease of memorization.

3. Surah 2:217 - Historical context of fighting during the sacred months.

4. Sahih Bukhari, Book 65, Hadith 1 - The significance of seeking knowledge.

C O N C L U S I O N

The Multidimensional Fabric of the Quran

The Quran, as a divine scripture, weaves together a rich tapestry of theological, ethical, social, and legal principles that have profoundly shaped the spiritual and worldly lives of Muslims. Its multifaceted teachings encompass every dimension of human existence, offering guidance that is both timeless and universally applicable. This comprehensive examination of the Quran's various aspects underscores its enduring relevance and transformative impact.

Theological and Ethical Foundations

At its core, the Quran establishes a profound theological framework, emphasizing the oneness of Allah (Tawhid) and the importance of faith, worship, and righteousness. Surah 112:1-4 encapsulates the essence of monotheism: "Say, 'He is Allah, [Who is] One, Allah, the Eternal Refuge. He neither begets nor is born, nor is there to Him any equivalent.'" This declaration of divine unity forms the bedrock of Islamic belief and practice.

The Quran's ethical teachings advocate for justice, compassion, and moral integrity. Surah 16:90 articulates a comprehensive ethical directive: "Indeed, Allah orders justice and good conduct and giving to relatives and forbids immorality and bad conduct and oppression. He admonishes you that perhaps you will be reminded." These principles guide personal conduct and social interactions, fostering a just and harmonious society.

Social Justice and Community Welfare

The Quran places significant emphasis on social justice and the welfare of the marginalized. The institution of Zakat, as outlined in Surah 9:60, mandates the redistribution of wealth to support the poor and needy: "Zakat expenditures are only for the poor and for the needy and for those employed to collect [Zakat] and for bringing hearts together [for Islam] and for freeing captives [or slaves] and for those in debt and for the cause of Allah and for the [stranded] traveler – an obligation [imposed] by Allah. And Allah is Knowing and Wise." This directive ensures economic equity and social solidarity.

The Hadith literature further reinforces the Quranic commitment to social welfare. In Sahih Muslim (Book 32, Hadith 6251), the Prophet Muhammad is reported to have said, "He who does not show mercy to others will not be shown mercy." This Hadith underscores the importance of compassion and empathy in community life, reflecting the ethical ethos of Islam.

Interfaith Relations and Universal Brotherhood

The Quran advocates for peaceful coexistence and respectful dialogue among different faith communities. Surah 2:256 asserts, "There is no compulsion in religion. The right course has become clear from the wrong." This verse underscores the principle of religious freedom and the importance of mutual respect.

The concept of universal brotherhood is central to the Quranic vision of social harmony. Surah 49:13 declares, "O mankind, indeed We have created you from male and female and made you peoples and tribes that you may know one another. Indeed, the most noble of you in the sight of Allah is the most righteous of you. Indeed, Allah is Knowing and Acquainted." This verse highlights the unity of humanity and the value of diversity.

Leadership and Governance

The Quran provides a framework for ethical leadership and governance, emphasizing justice, consultation (Shura), and accountability. Surah 4:58 instructs, "Indeed, Allah commands you to render trusts to whom they are due and when you judge between people to judge with justice. Excellent is that which Allah instructs you. Indeed, Allah is ever Hearing and Seeing." This verse underscores the principles of trust and justice that are essential for effective governance.

The Hadith literature elaborates on these principles. In Sahih Bukhari (Book 92, Hadith 30), it is narrated that the Prophet Muhammad frequently consulted his companions, exemplifying the Quranic principle of inclusive decision-making. This practice of Shura ensures that leadership is participatory and grounded in collective wisdom.

Environmental Stewardship and Health

The Quran advocates for environmental stewardship and the conservation of natural resources. Surah 6:165 emphasizes the role of humanity as stewards of the Earth: "And it is He who has made you successors upon the earth." This verse highlights the responsibility to protect and preserve the natural environment.

Health and wellness are also integral to the Quranic vision of a balanced life. The Hadith literature provides practical guidance on health, diet, and hygiene, promoting a holistic approach to well-being. In Sahih Muslim (Book 2, Hadith 496), the Prophet Muhammad is reported to have said, "Do not waste water, even if you perform your ablution on the banks of an abundantly-flowing river." This Hadith underscores the importance of conserving vital resources.

Conclusion

The Quran offers a multidimensional blueprint for a just, compassionate, and ethical society. Its teachings encompass every aspect of human life, providing guidance that is both spiritually profound and practically applicable. The Hadith literature complements and enriches the Quranic message, offering detailed expositions and practical applications of its principles.

By adhering to the Quranic teachings, individuals and communities can aspire to achieve a higher standard of moral and ethical integrity, fostering a world characterized by justice, compassion, and harmony. This holistic vision reflects the timeless relevance of the Quran as a divine guide for all of humanity.

References:

1. Surah 112:1-4 - Declaration of divine unity.

2. Surah 16:90 - Comprehensive ethical directive.

3. Surah 9:60 - Redistribution of wealth through Zakat.

4. Sahih Muslim, Book 32, Hadith 6251 - Importance of compassion and empathy.

5. Surah 2:256 - Principle of religious freedom.

6. Surah 49:13 - Unity of humanity and value of diversity.

7. Surah 4:58 - Principles of trust and justice in governance.

8. Sahih Bukhari, Book 92, Hadith 30 - Inclusive decision-making through consultation.

9. Surah 6:165 - Humanity's role as stewards of the Earth.

10. Sahih Muslim, Book 2, Hadith 496 - Conservation of resources.

9 798348 201579